AF489051

How to Draw Cartoon Dinosaurs for Kids (Step by step instructions on how to draw 38 dinosaurs)

This book has over 300 detailed illustrations that demonstrate how to draw dinosaurs step by step

J.P. Manning

Copyright © 2020

All rights reserved. No part of this publication may be reproduced, stored in a retrieval system, or transmitted in any form or by any means, electronic, mechanical, recording, scanning, or otherwise, except as permitted under copyright legislation, without the prior permission of the authors.

Limits of liability/disclaimer of warranty –

The authors have used their best efforts in preparing this book, they make no representations or warranties with respect to the accuracy or the completeness of the contents of this book and specifically disclaim any implied warranties or merchantability or fitness for a particular purpose. No warranty may be created or extended. The author shall not be liable for any loss or profit or any other commercial damages, including but not limited to special, incidental, consequential or other damages.

Copyright © 2020

1. How to draw a flying dinosaur. Begin by drawing a basic grid. This grid will help you to line up the dinosaur's eyes with its beak.

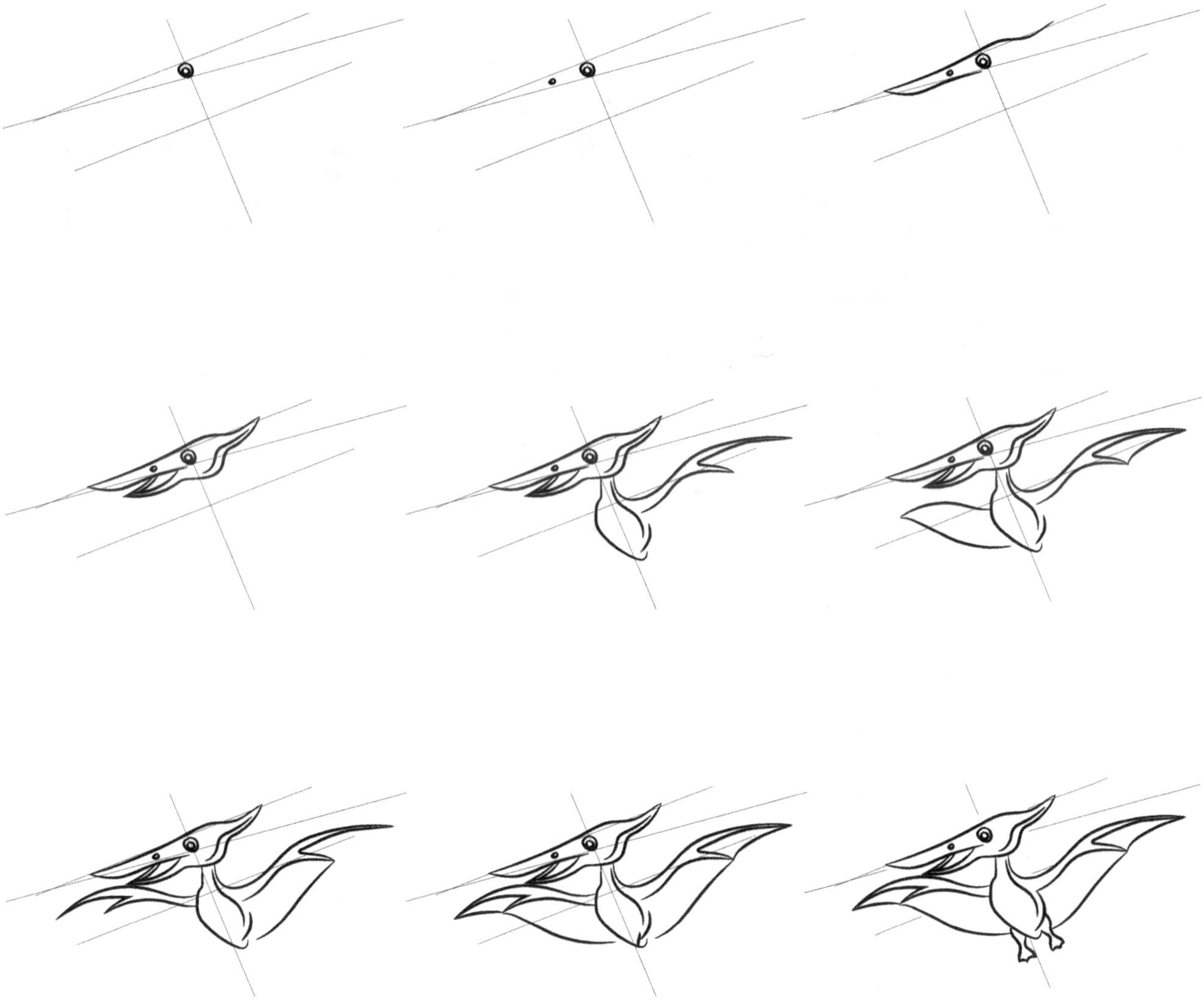

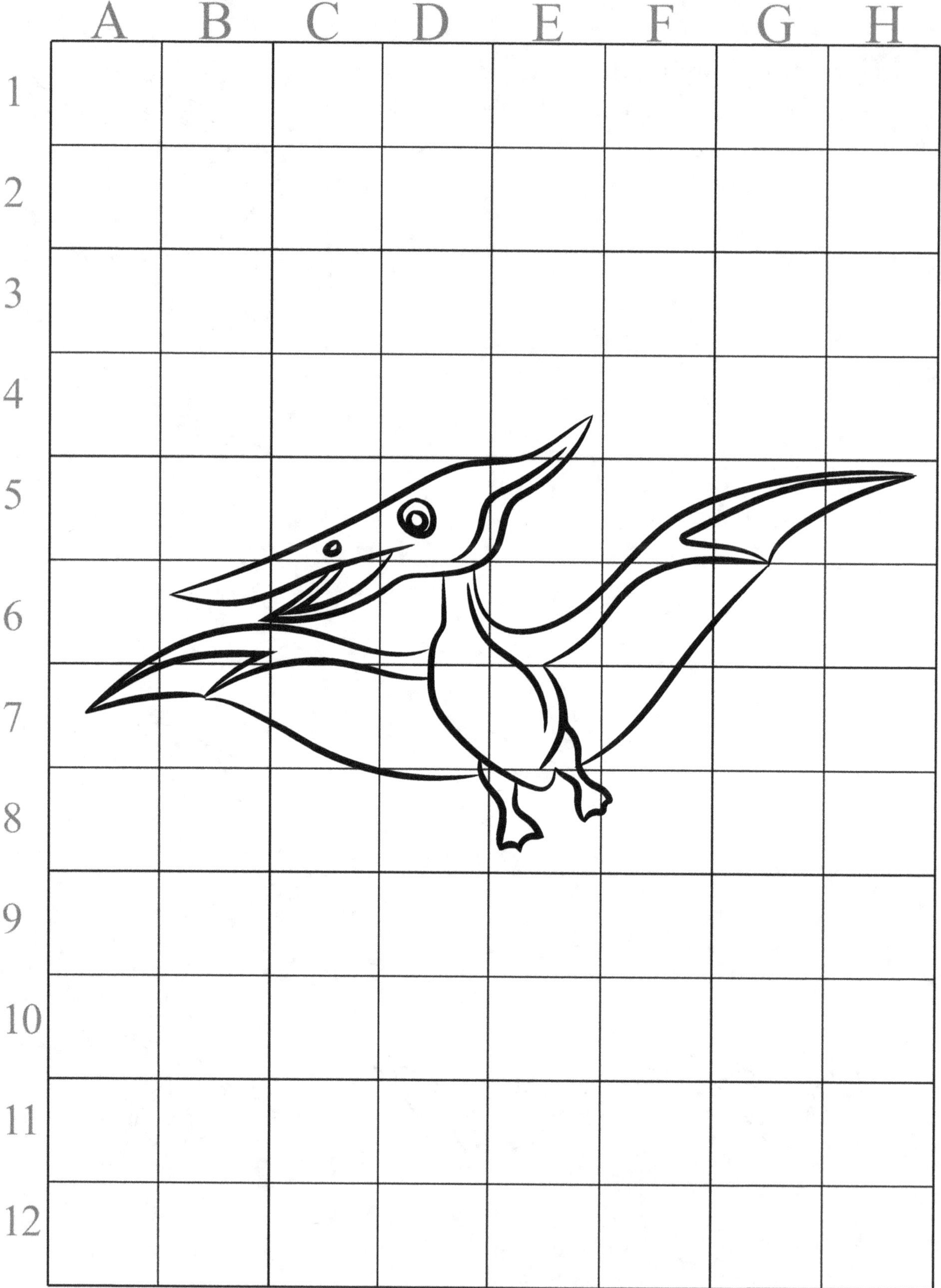

A B C D E F G H
1
2
3
4
5
6
7
8
9
10
11
12

2. How to draw a standing dinosaur. Draw a basic grid with rough outlines of the dinosaur's head and its body. This grid is approximate and does not need to be exact.

A B C D E F G H
1
2
3
4
5
6
7
8
9
10
11
12

3. How to draw a dinosaur. Begin by drawing
a basic grid. This will help you to keep your
picture in proportion. Parallel lines where
you intend to place the dinosaur's eyes can
also be very helpful.

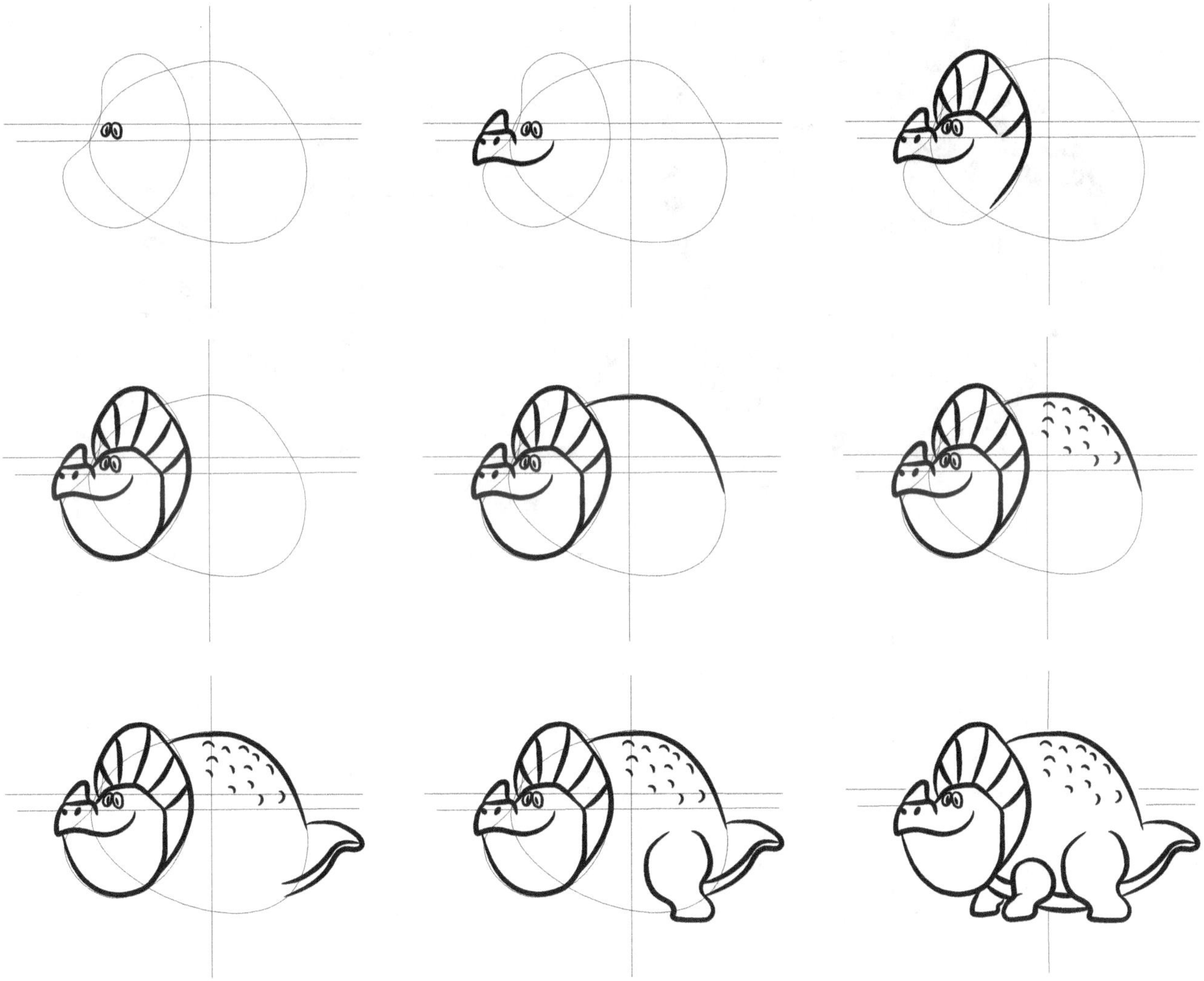

A B C D E F G H
1
2
3
4
5
6
7
8
9
10
11
12

4. How to draw a dinosaur. Begin by drawing a grid. Create two parallel lines as guides for your eyes. Sketching two further ellipses as guides will help you maintain the proportions of the head and the body.

A B C D E F G H
1
2
3
4
5
6
7
8
9
10
11
12

5. How to draw a stegosaurus. You can create a basic grid pattern to guide you in drawing a stegosaurus.

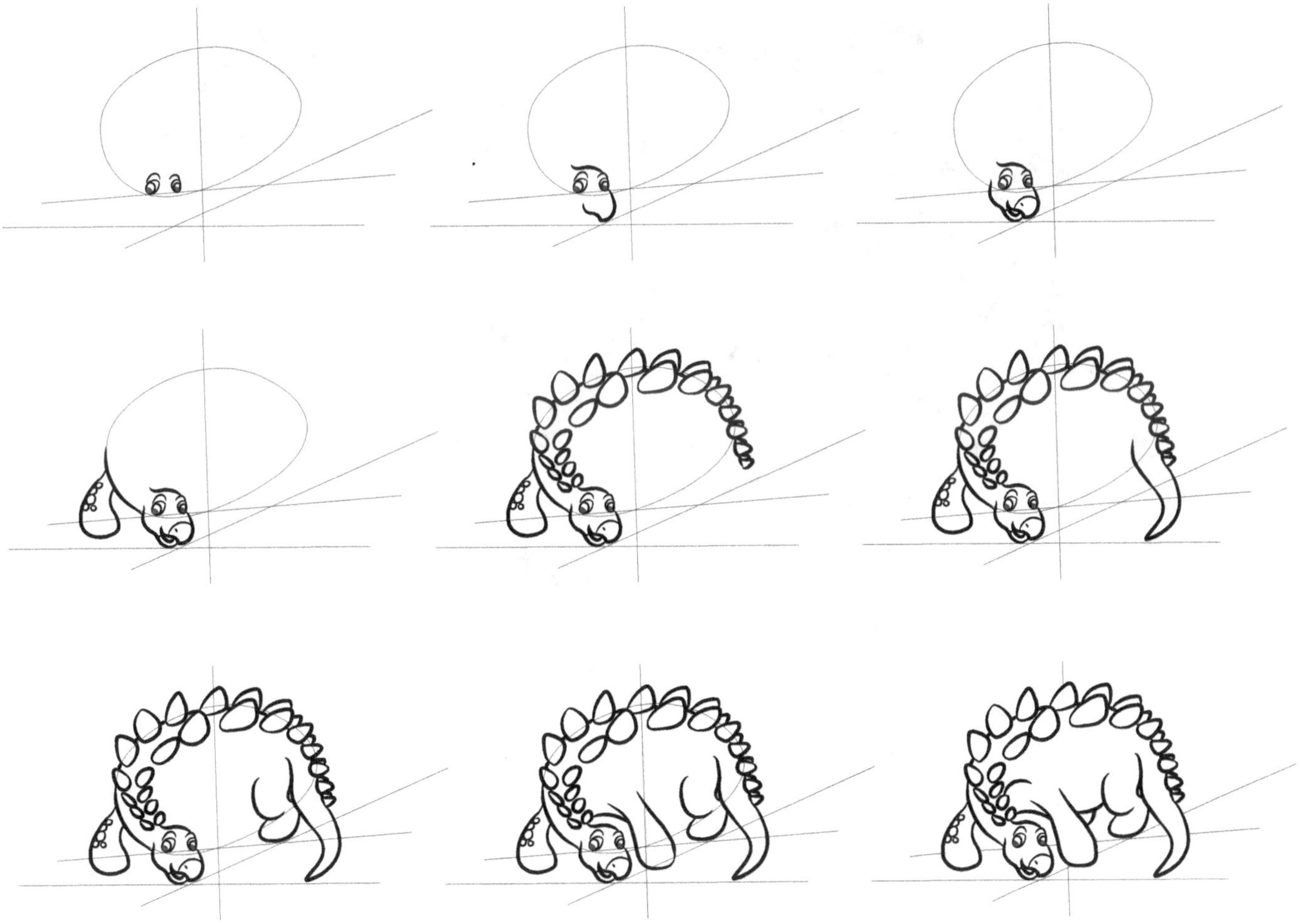

A B C D E F G H
1
2
3
4
5
6
7
8
9
10
11
12

6. How to draw a two-legged dinosaur. A basic grid can help you to keep your drawing in proportion. Two parallel lines for the dinosaur's eyes will also help.

7. How to draw a simple t-rex. Draw a basic grid to help you with this. Use two ellipses to help you decide where to put the head and the body.

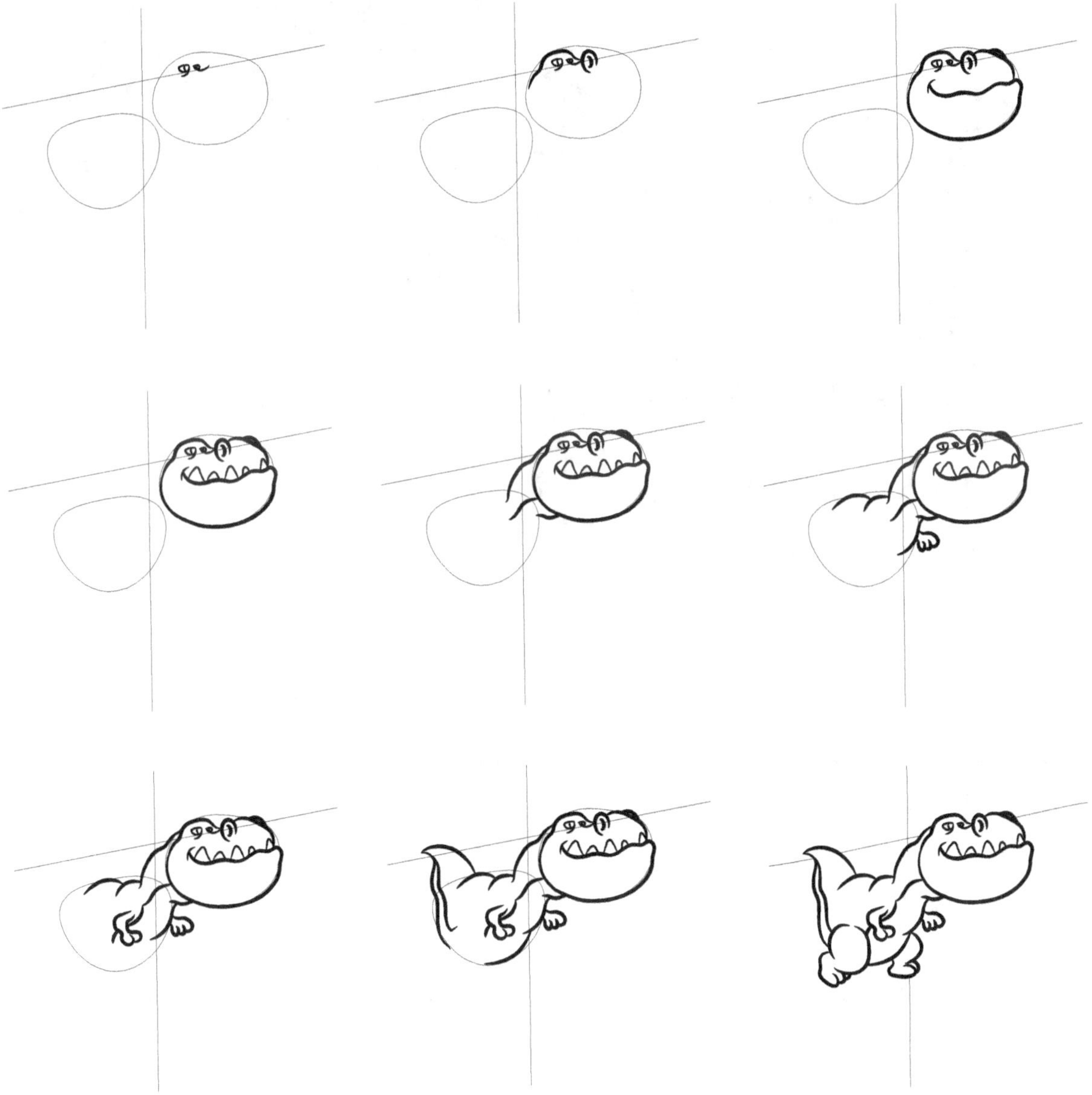

8. How to draw a Dinosaur. Start with a basic grid. Drawing the eyes first will help you to decide where other parts of your dinosaur need to be.

A B C D E F G H
1
2
3
4
5
6
7
8
9
10
11
12

9. How to draw a dinosaur. After drawing your grid, start with your dinosaur's eyes. You can follow this with a basic head shape.

A B C D E F G H
1
2
3
4
5
6
7
8
9
10
11
12

10. How to draw a winged standing dinosaur. A simple grid will help you to keep things in proportion.

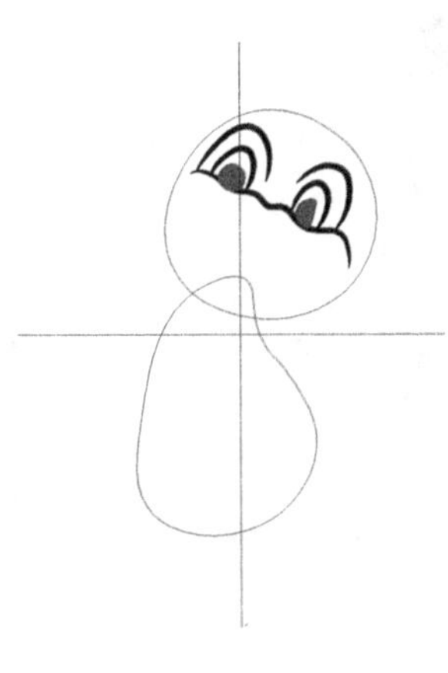

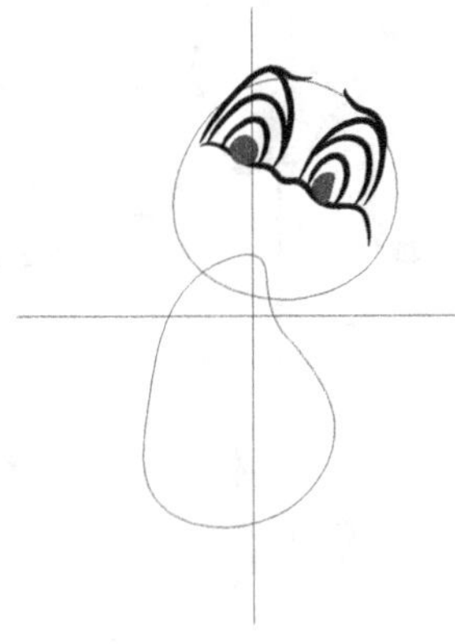

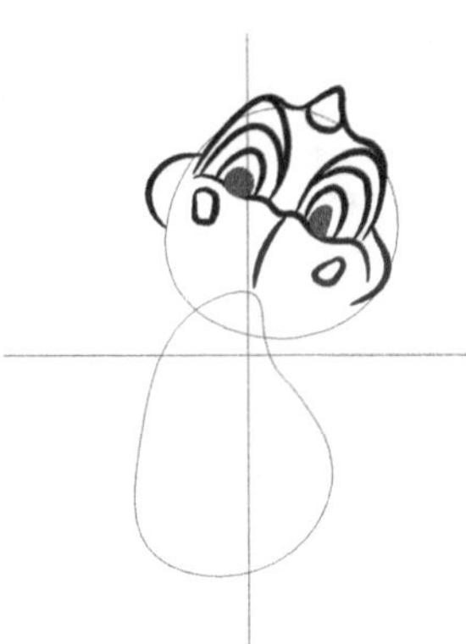

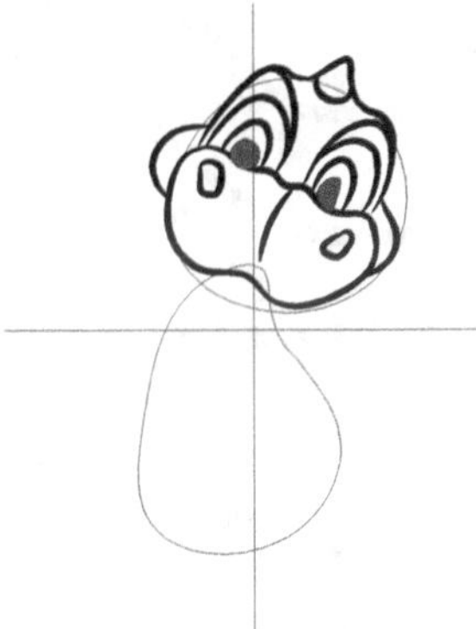

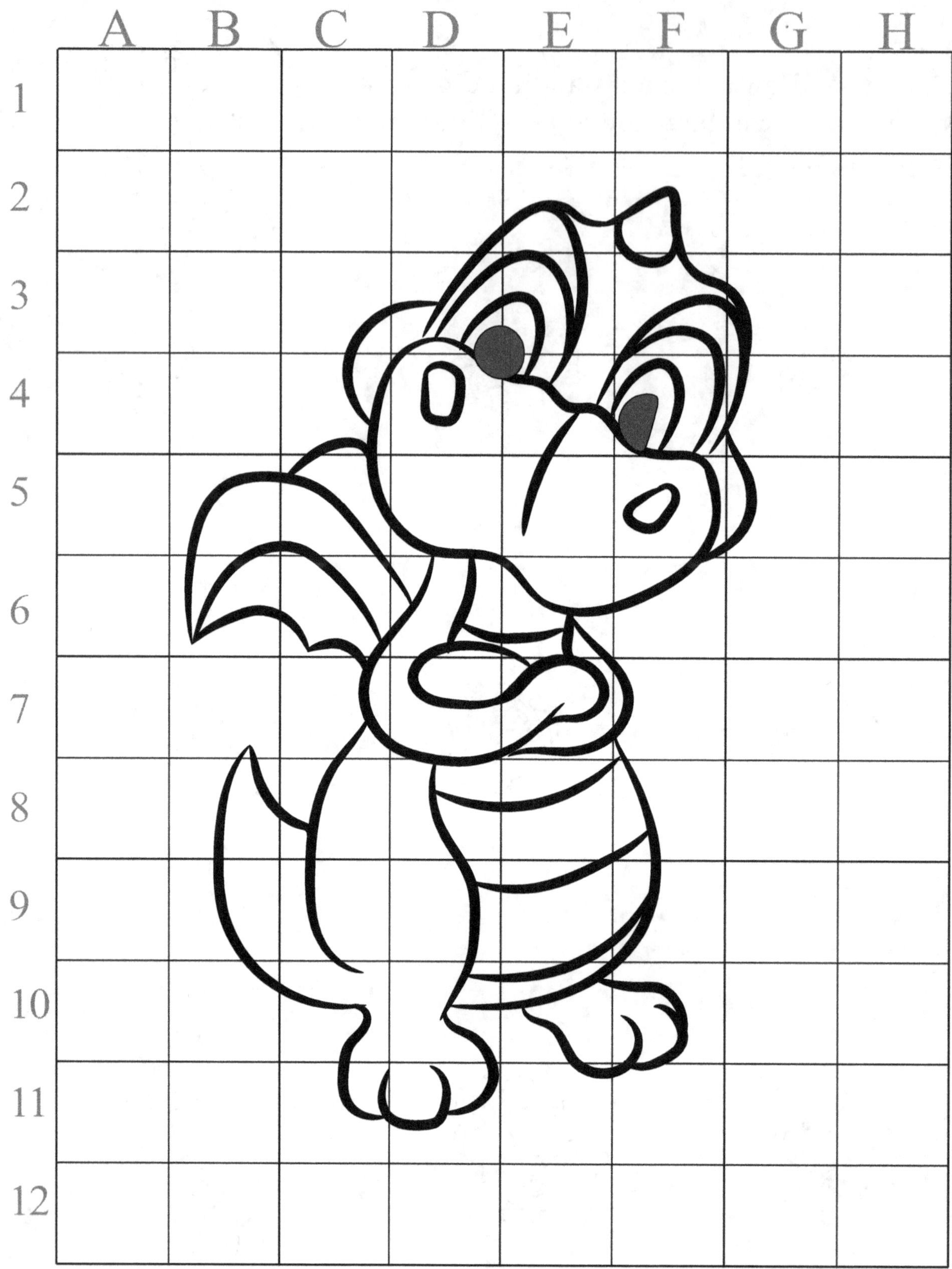

11. How to draw a dinosaur. Adding one section of your dinosaur at a time will make your drawing project feel less overwhelming.

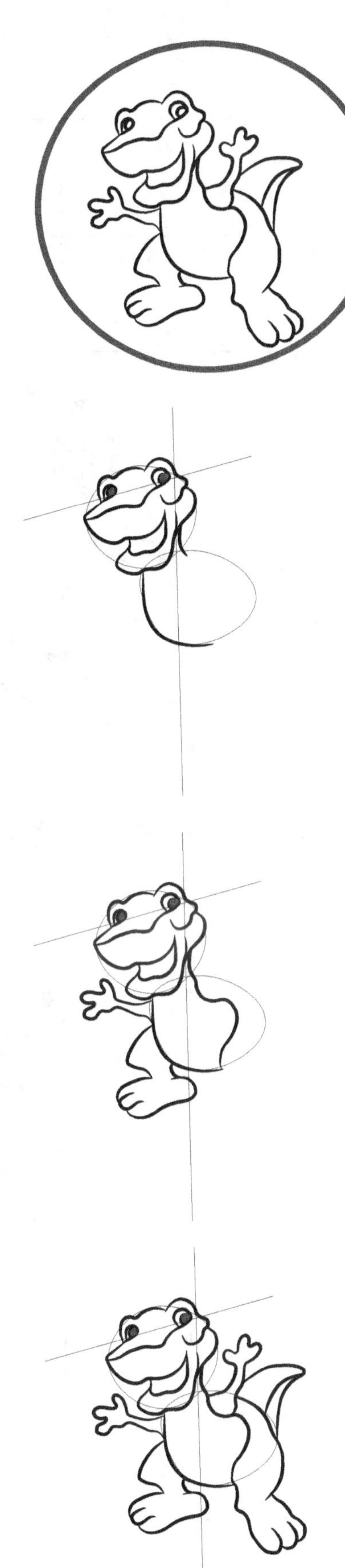

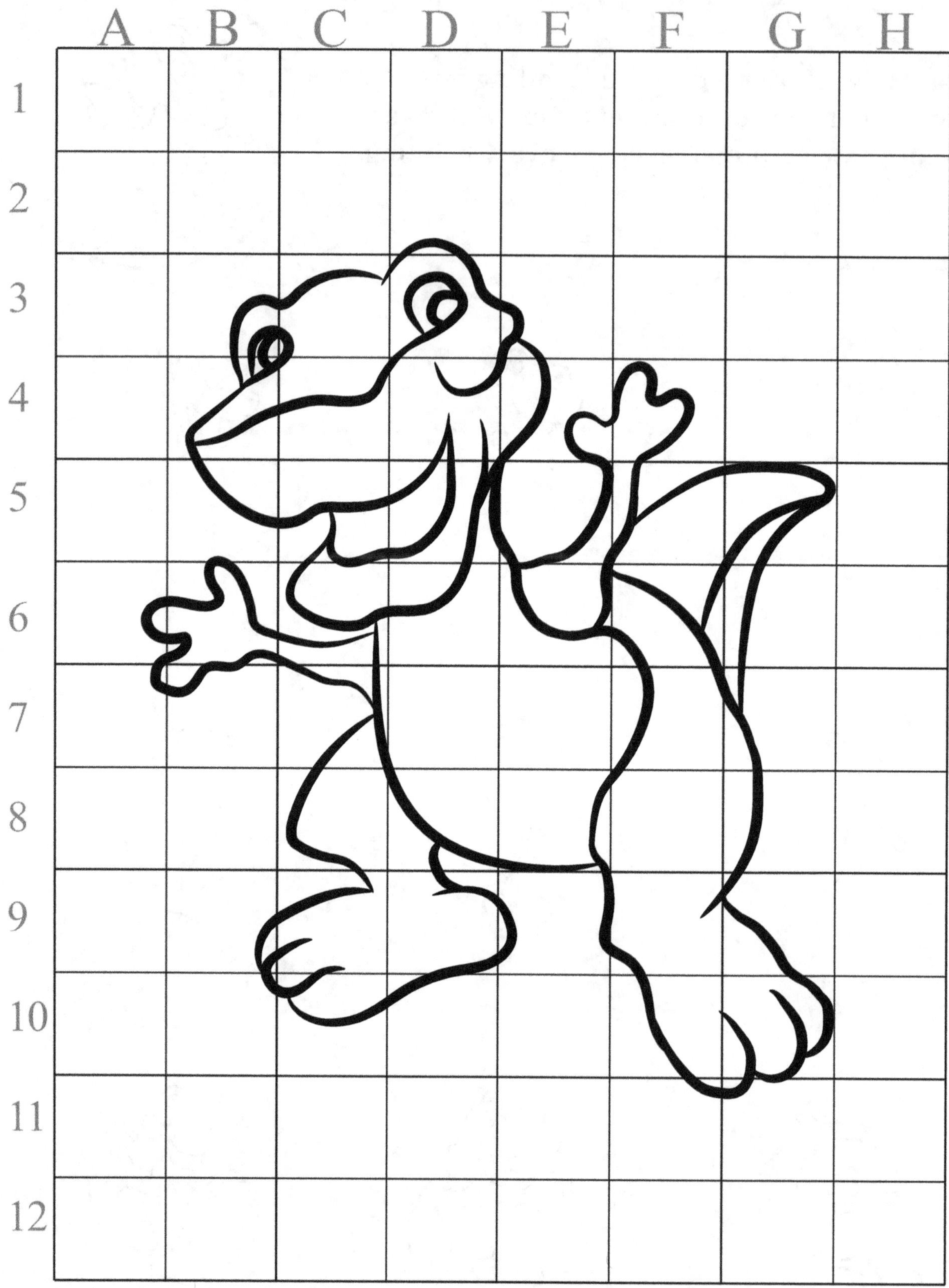

A B C D E F G H
1
2
3
4
5
6
7
8
9
10
11
12

12. How to draw a dinosaur. A basic grid will help you to easily organise your drawing.

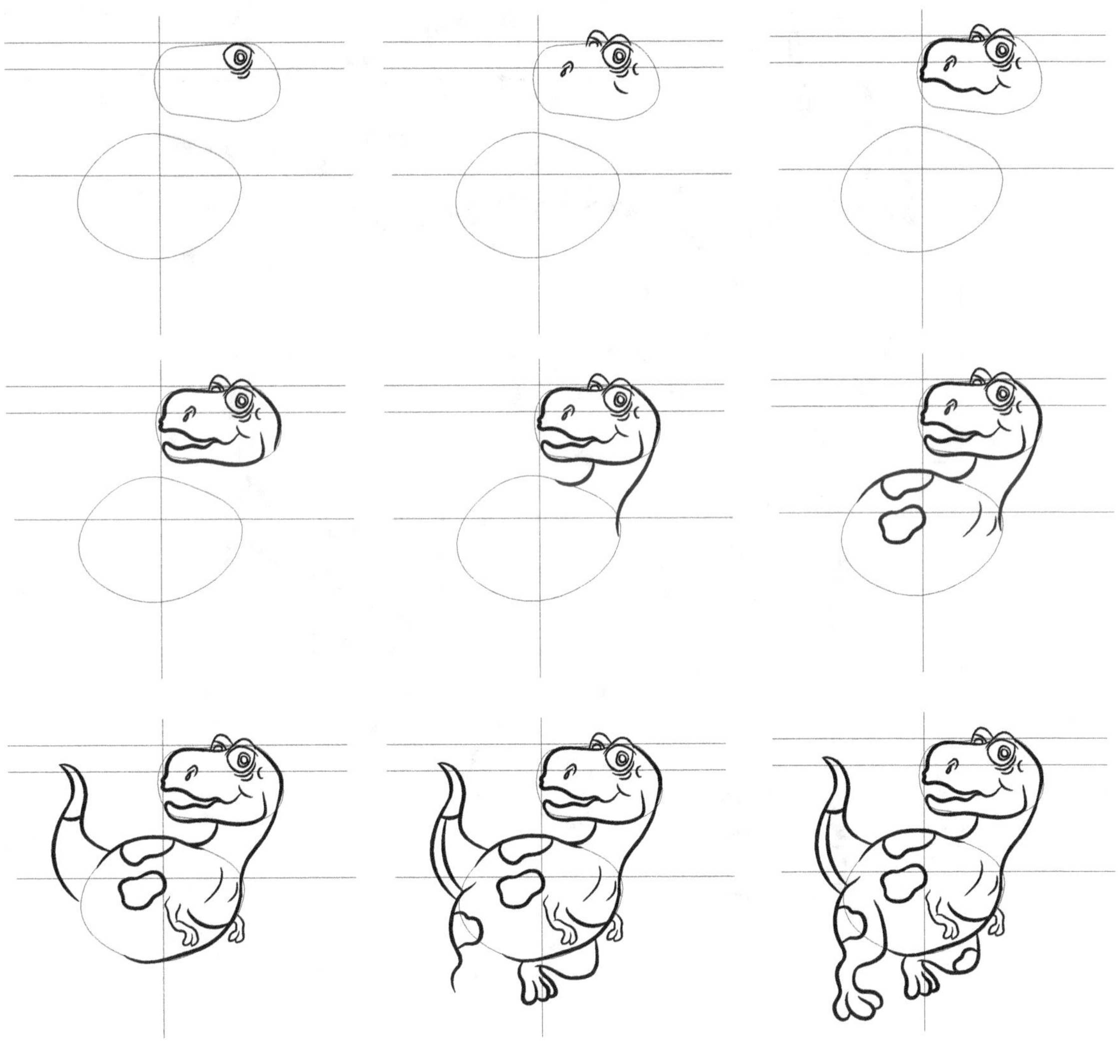

A B C D E F G H
1
2
3
4
5
6
7
8
9
10
11
12

13. How to draw a flying dinosaur. A simple grid can often help to guide you on drawing your dinosaur's wings.

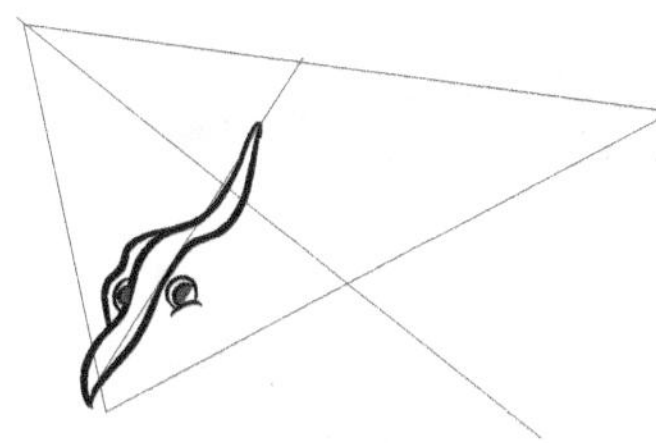  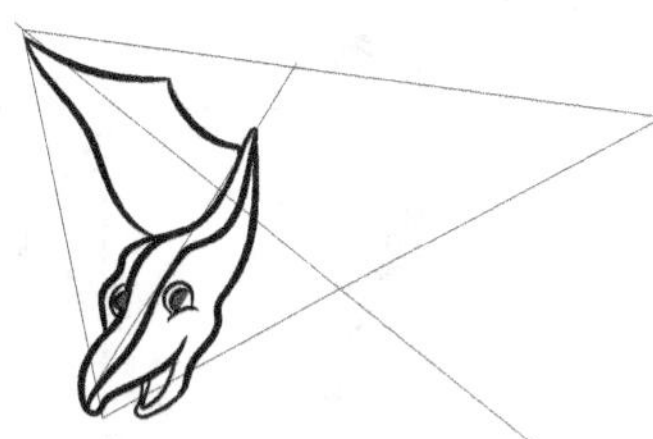

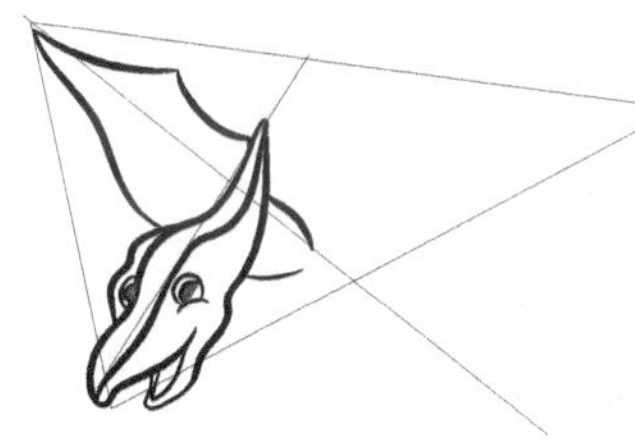 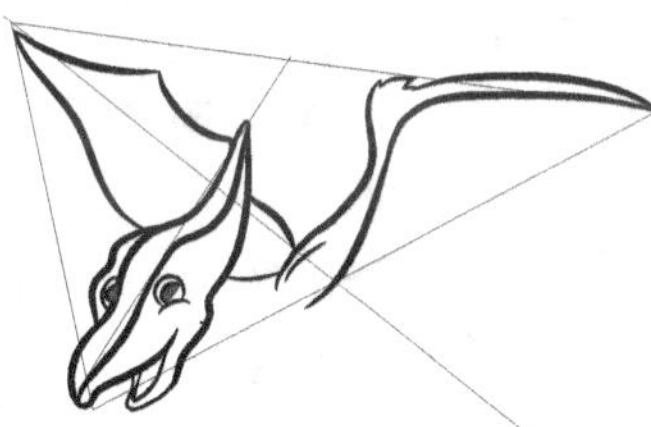 

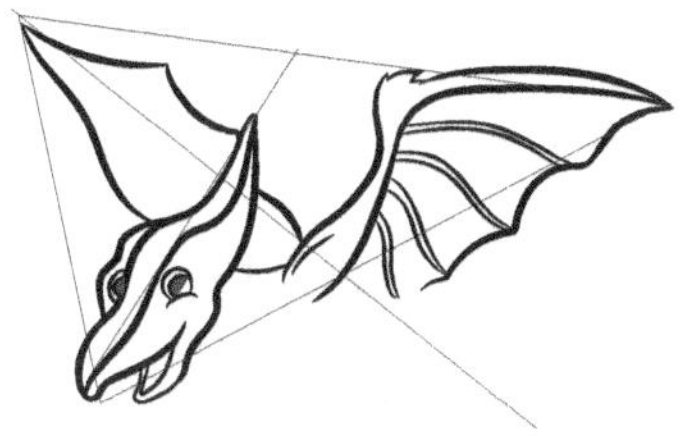  

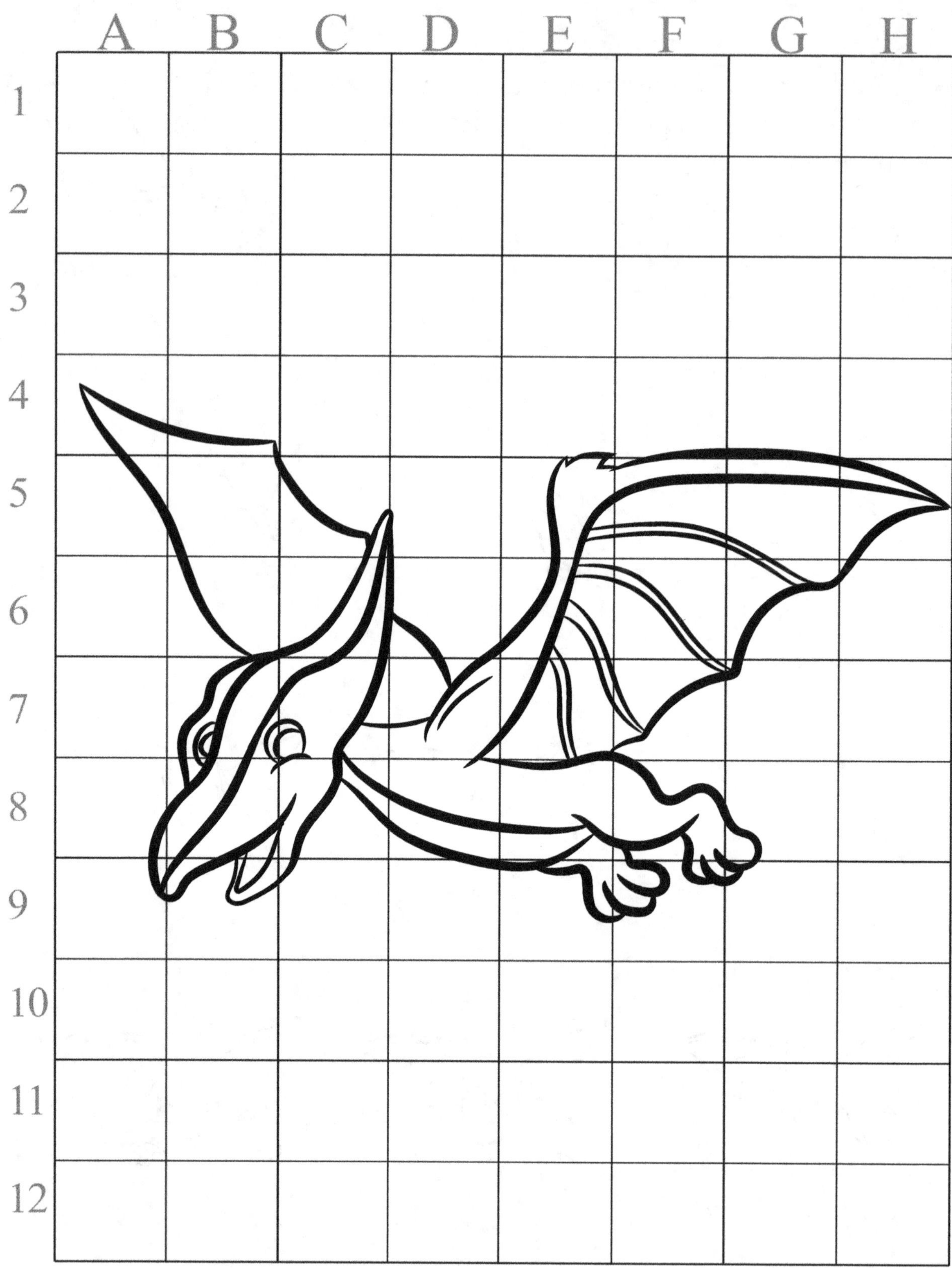

A B C D E F G H
1
2
3
4
5
6
7
8
9
10
11
12

14. How to draw a dinosaur. Here we will be working on a profile. Two parallel lines drawn through the centre of your grid will help you with the positioning of your dinosaur's eye and keep the eye in line with the body.

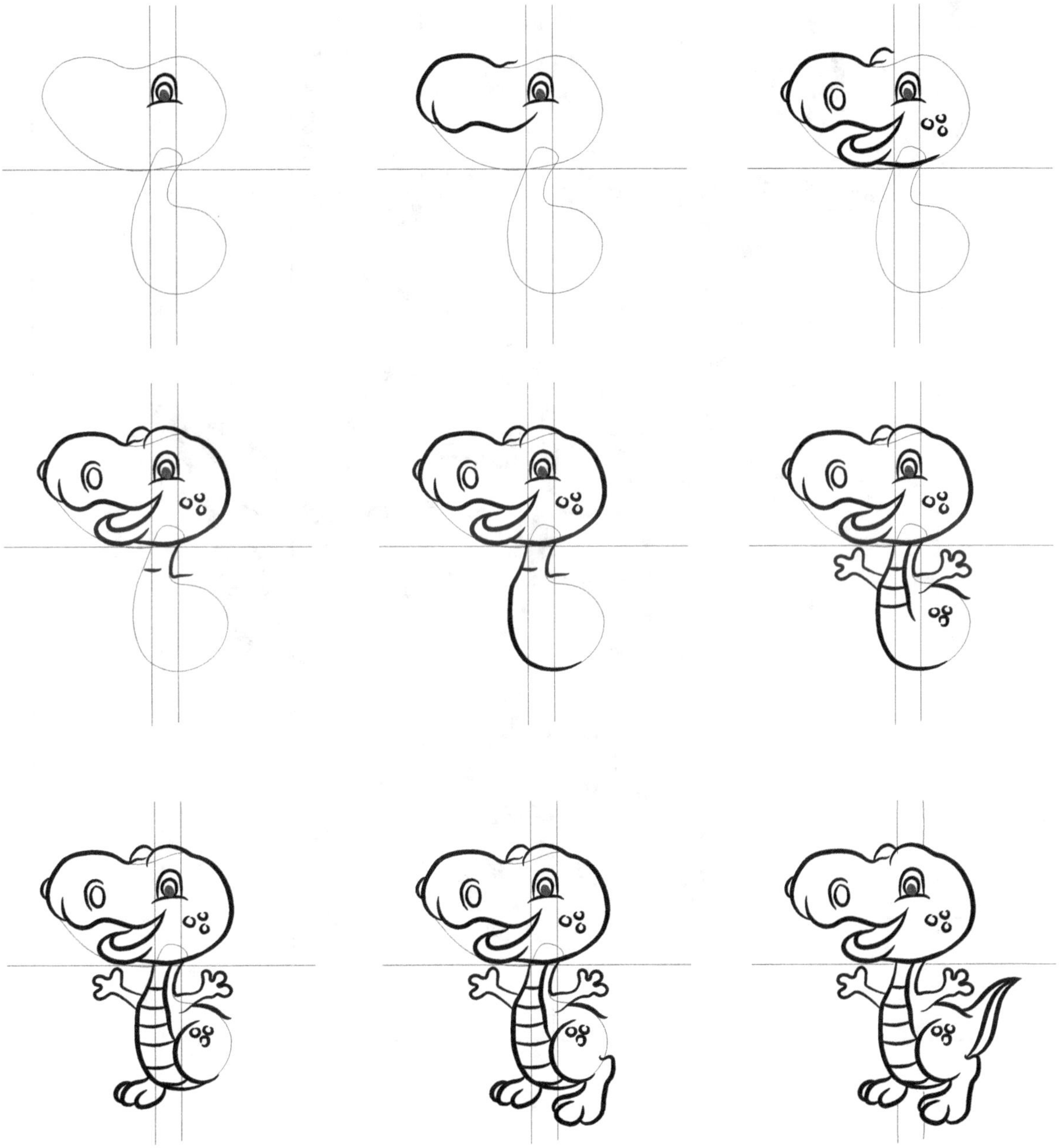

15. How to draw a dinosaur. Drawing lines for the eyes in your initial grid will help you to keep the sizes of your dinosaur's eyes in proportion.

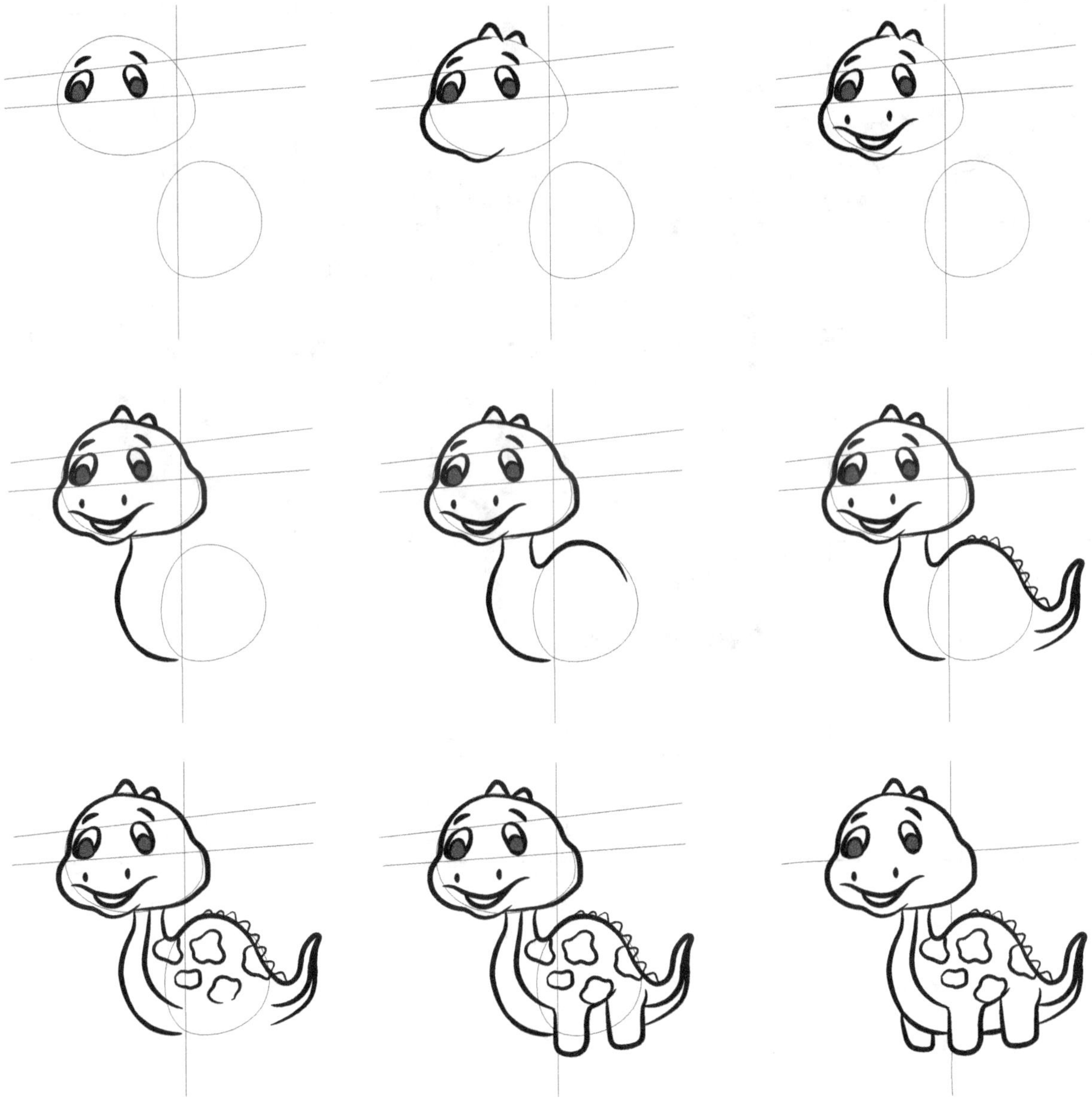

A B C D E F G H
1 2 3 4 5 6 7 8 9 10 11 12

16. How to draw a two-legged dinosaur in profile. Begin by drawing your basic grid. Following this start by drawing your dinosaur's eye and build the rest of your picture around it.

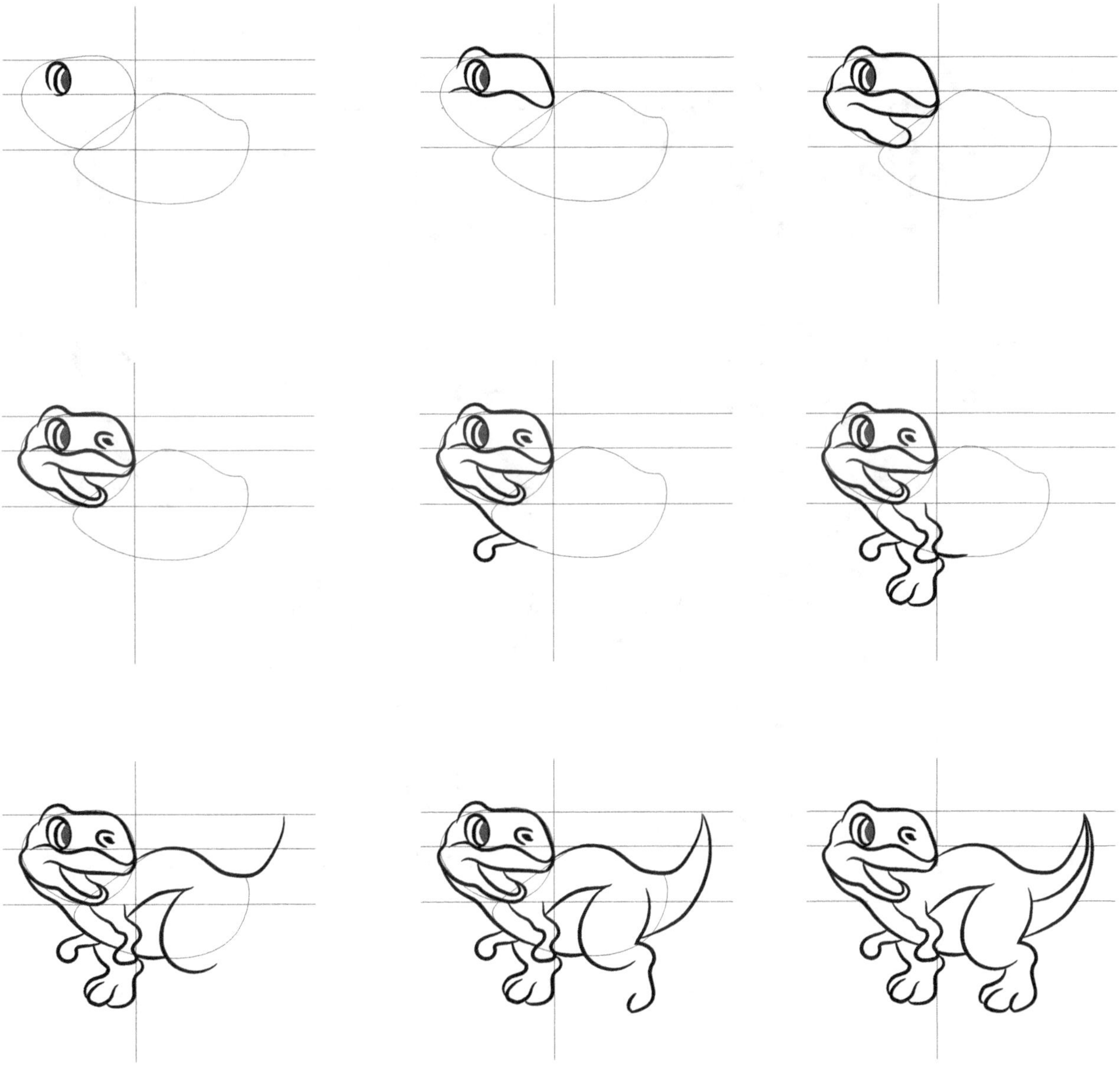

A B C D E F G H
1
2
3
4
5
6
7
8
9
10
11
12

17. How to draw a dinosaur. When you want your dinosaur's head to be more dominant you can sketch two overlapping ellipses in your grid. Just make sure the ellipse for the head is much larger.

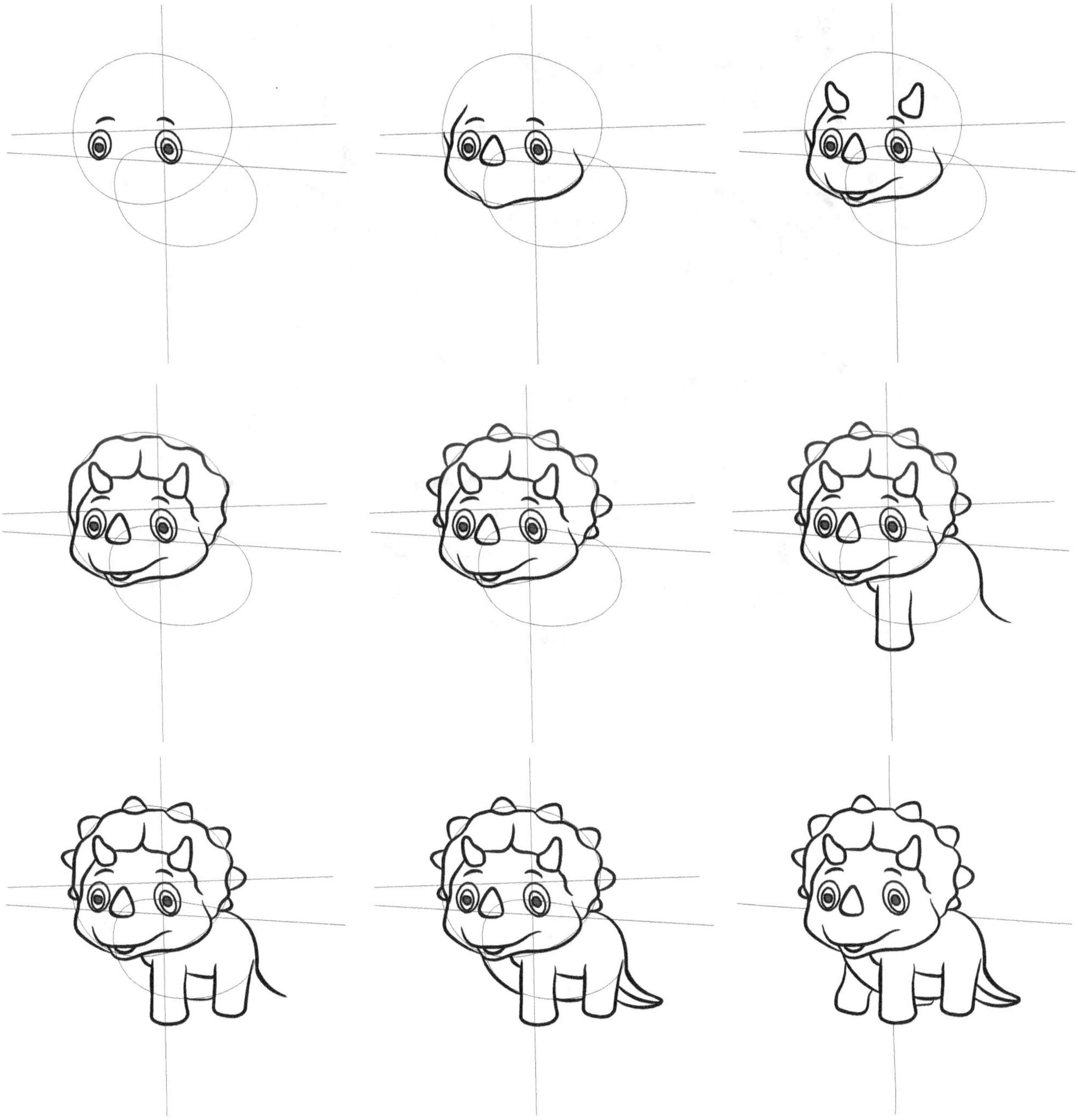

18. How to draw a Parasaur. Sketch out a basic grid first to keep your dinosaur in proportion. Start by drawing the eyes and construct the rest of your picture around them.

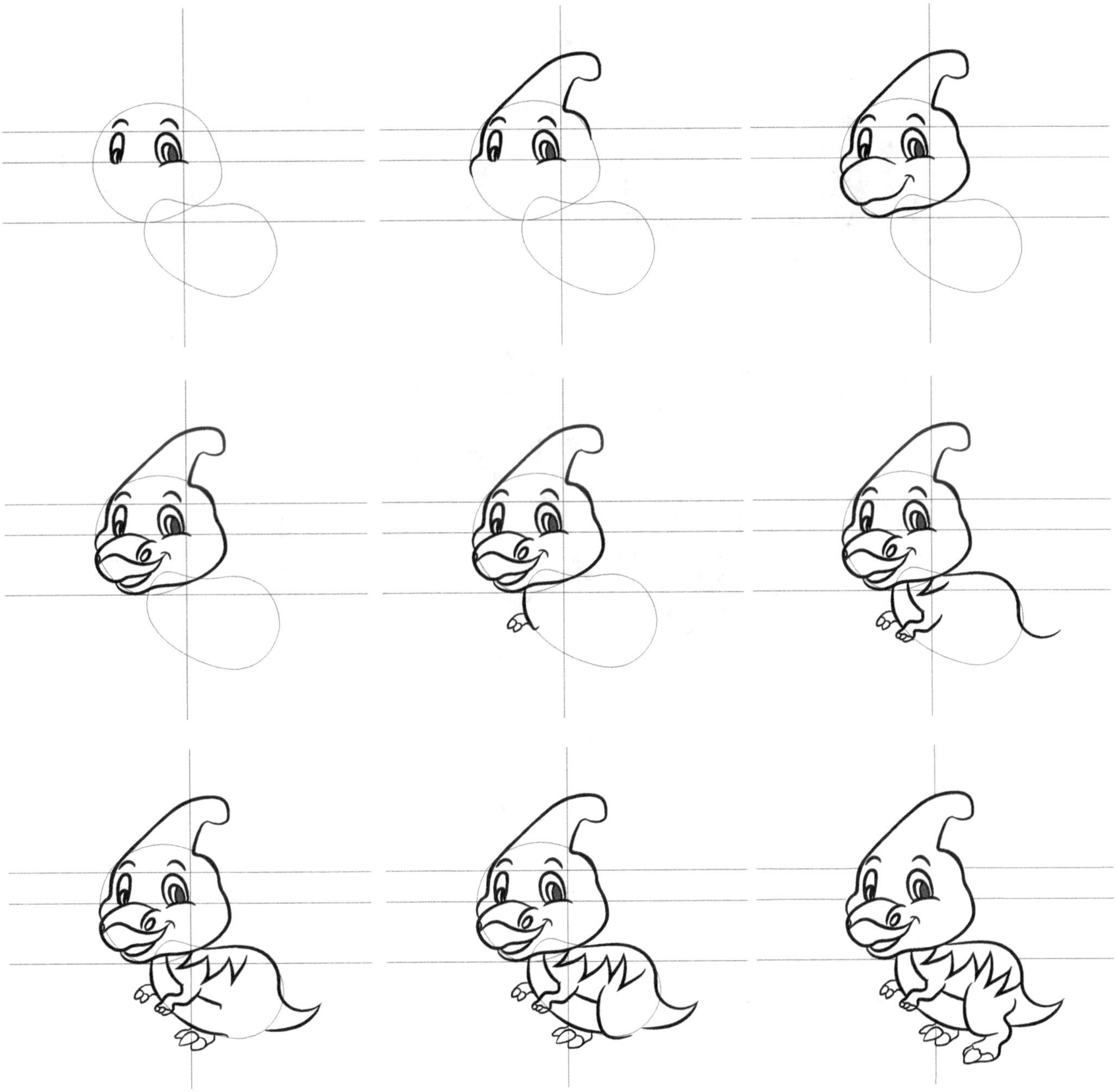

A B C D E F G H
1
2
3
4
5
6
7
8
9
10
11
12

19. How to draw a dinosaur. Sometimes adding a triangular shape to your basic grid can help to keep your dinosaur's body in line.

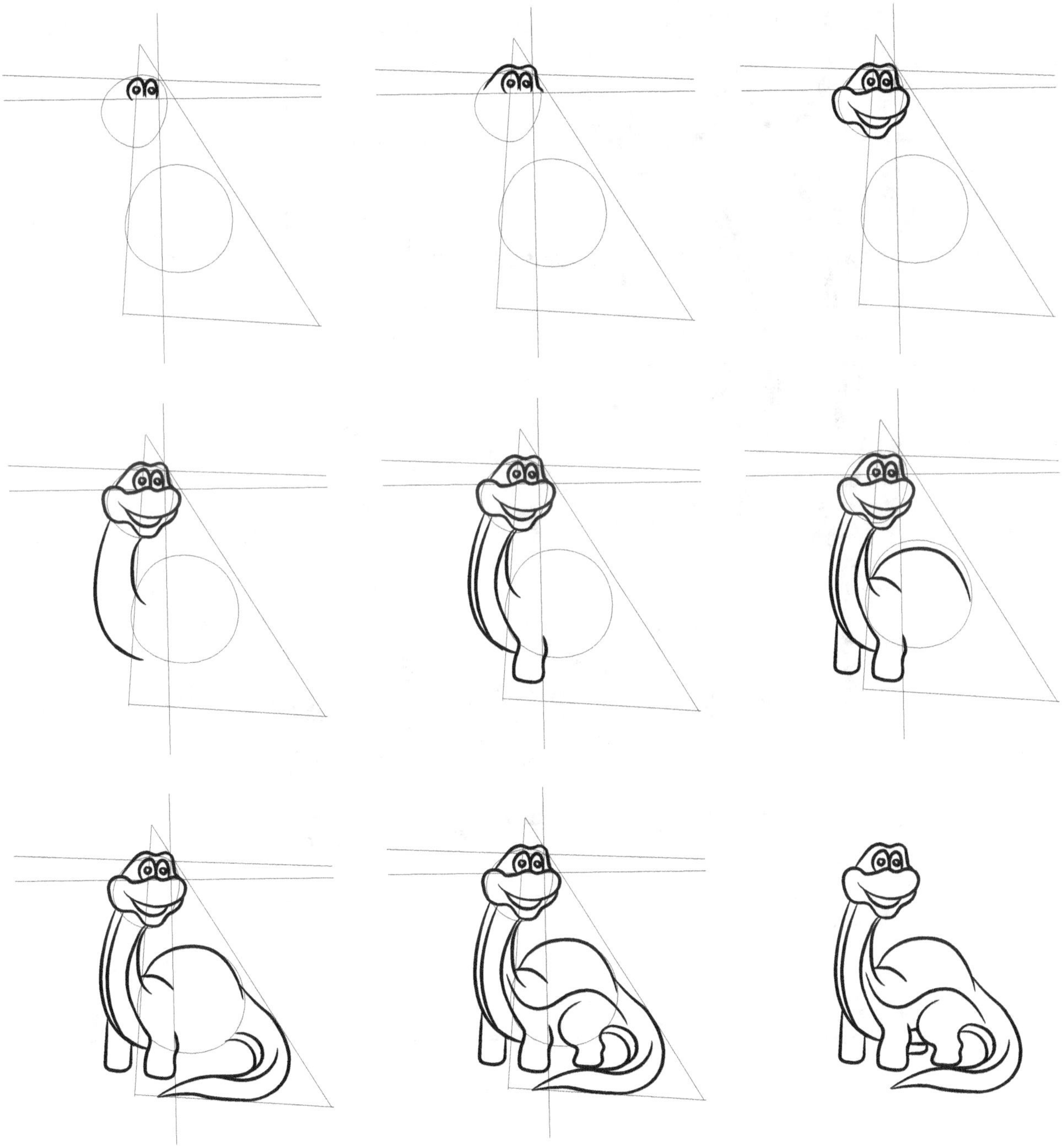

A B C D E F G H
1
2
3
4
5
6
7
8
9
10
11
12

20. How to draw a dinosaur. Drawing a triangle
in your grid can be used to remind yourself
about where your dinosaur is looking.

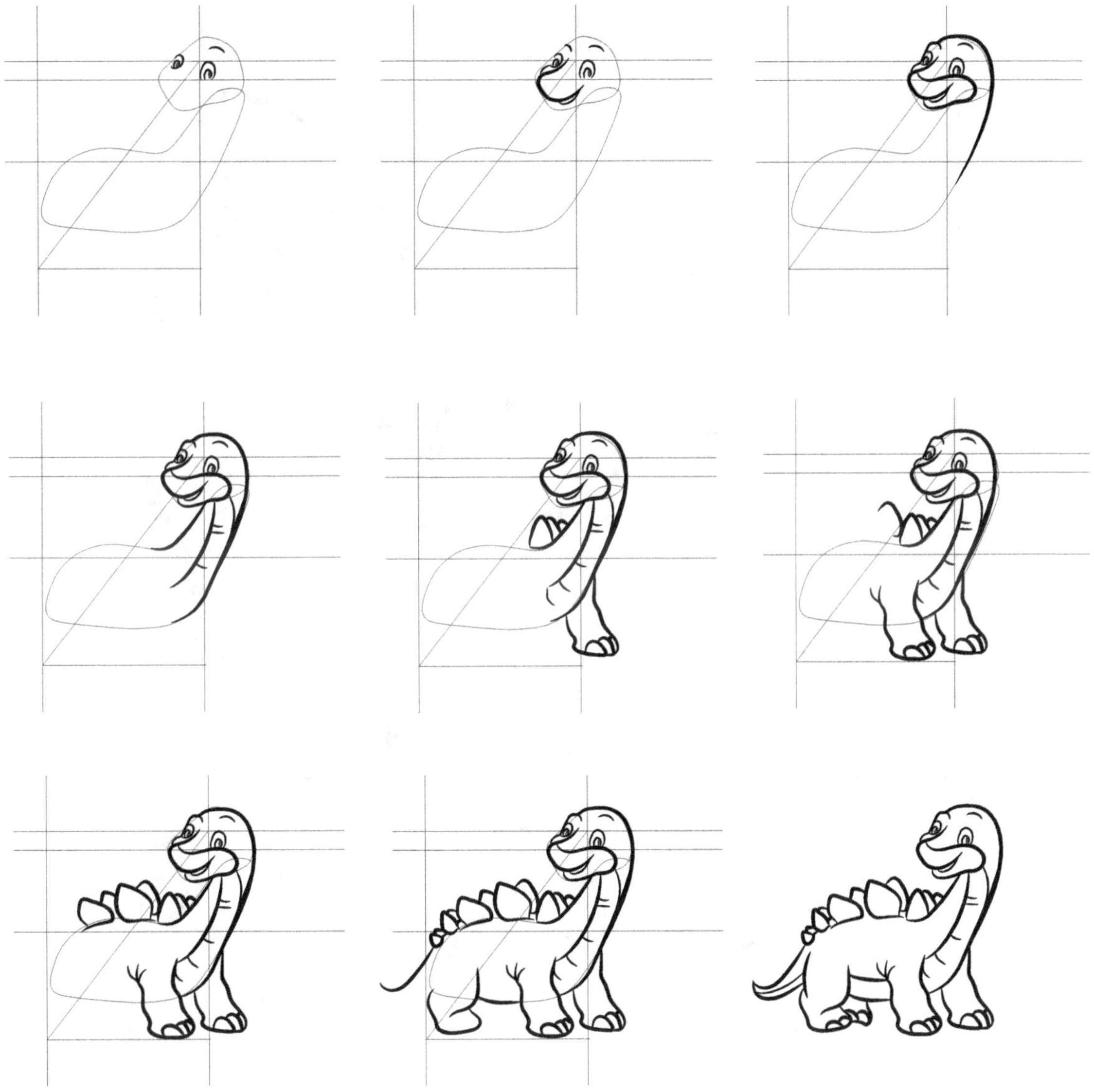

A B C D E F G H
1
2
3
4
5
6
7
8
9
10
11
12

21. How to draw a dinosaur. The use of ellipses can be very helpful, especially when deciding where to place the head and the body.

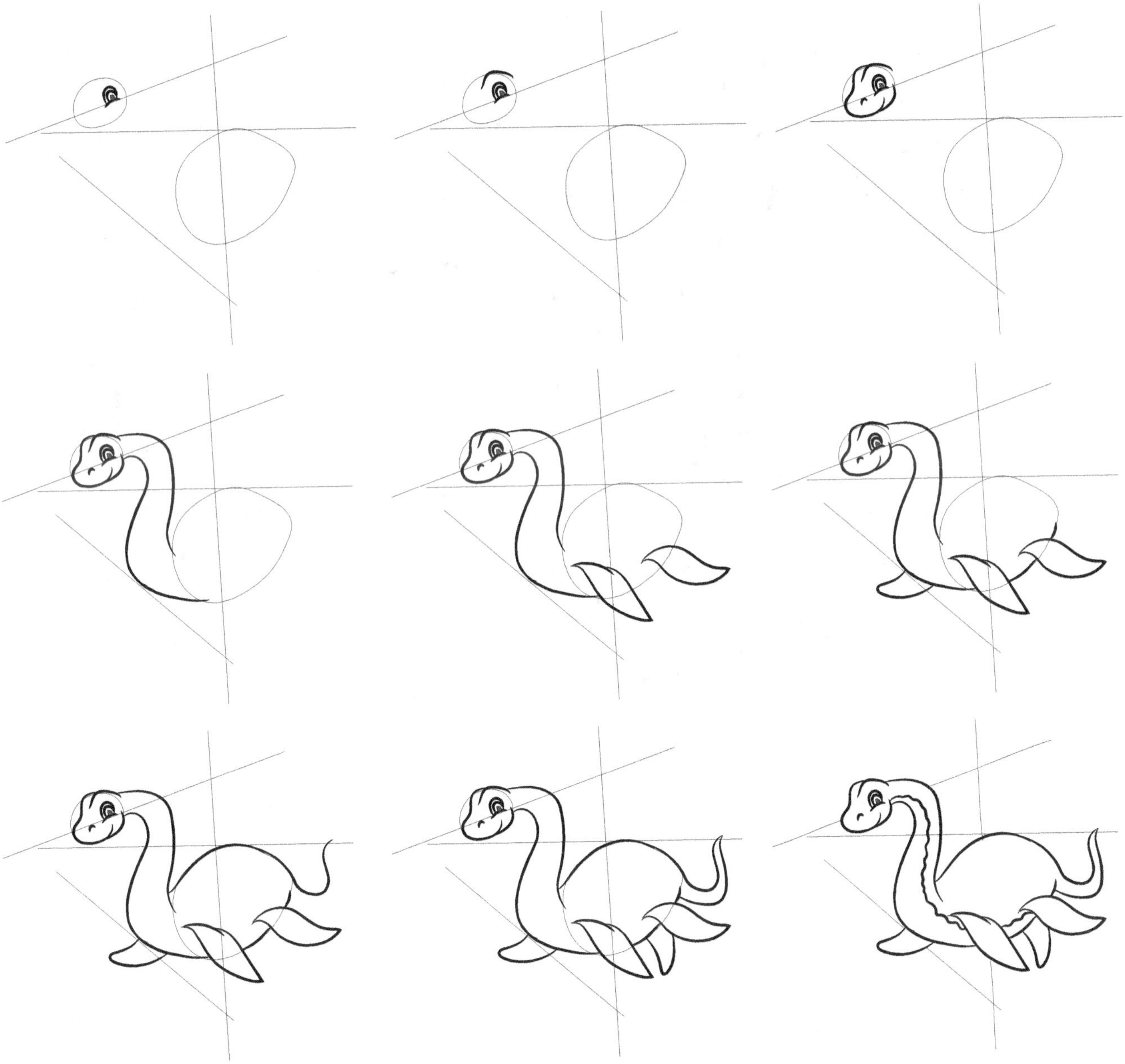

A B C D E F G H
1
2
3
4
5
6
7
8
9
10
11
12

22. How to draw a dinosaur with a long neck. Draw two ellipses after you have decided where to place the head and the body. Begin by drawing the eyes and the head.

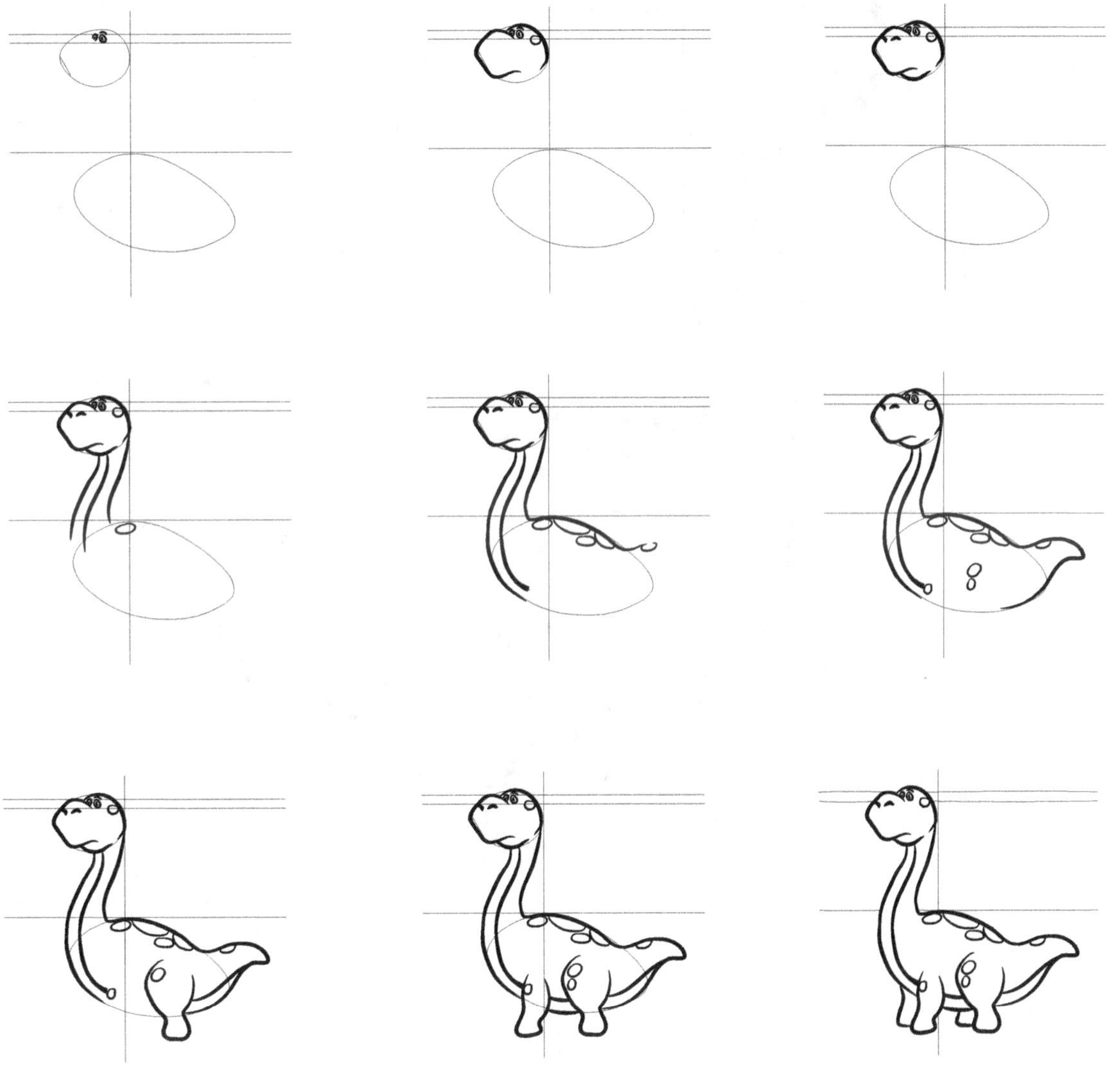

A B C D E F G H
1
2
3
4
5
6
7
8
9
10
11
12

23. How to draw a dinosaur. You can change the size of your dinosaur's body by altering the size of your ellipse.

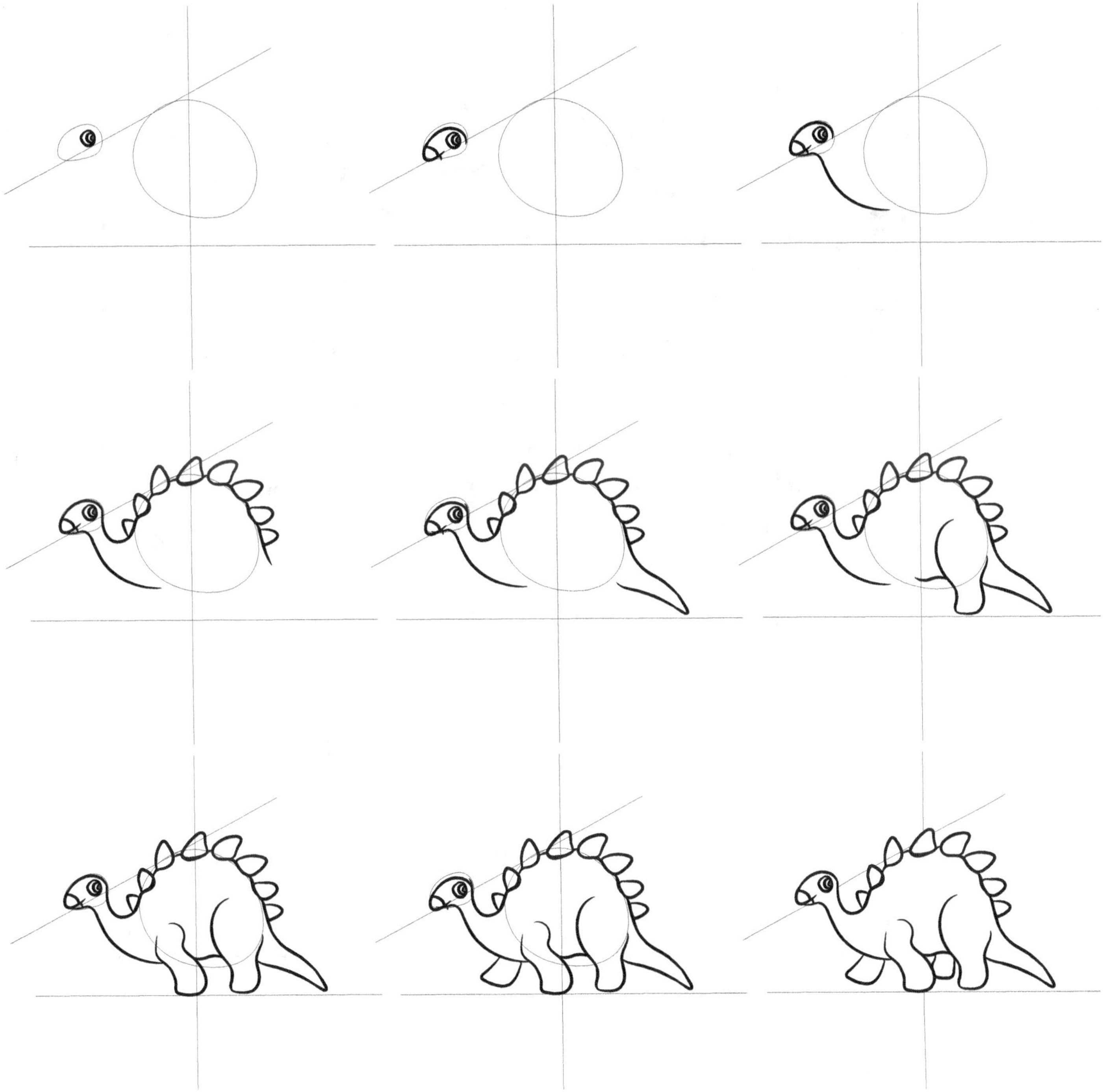

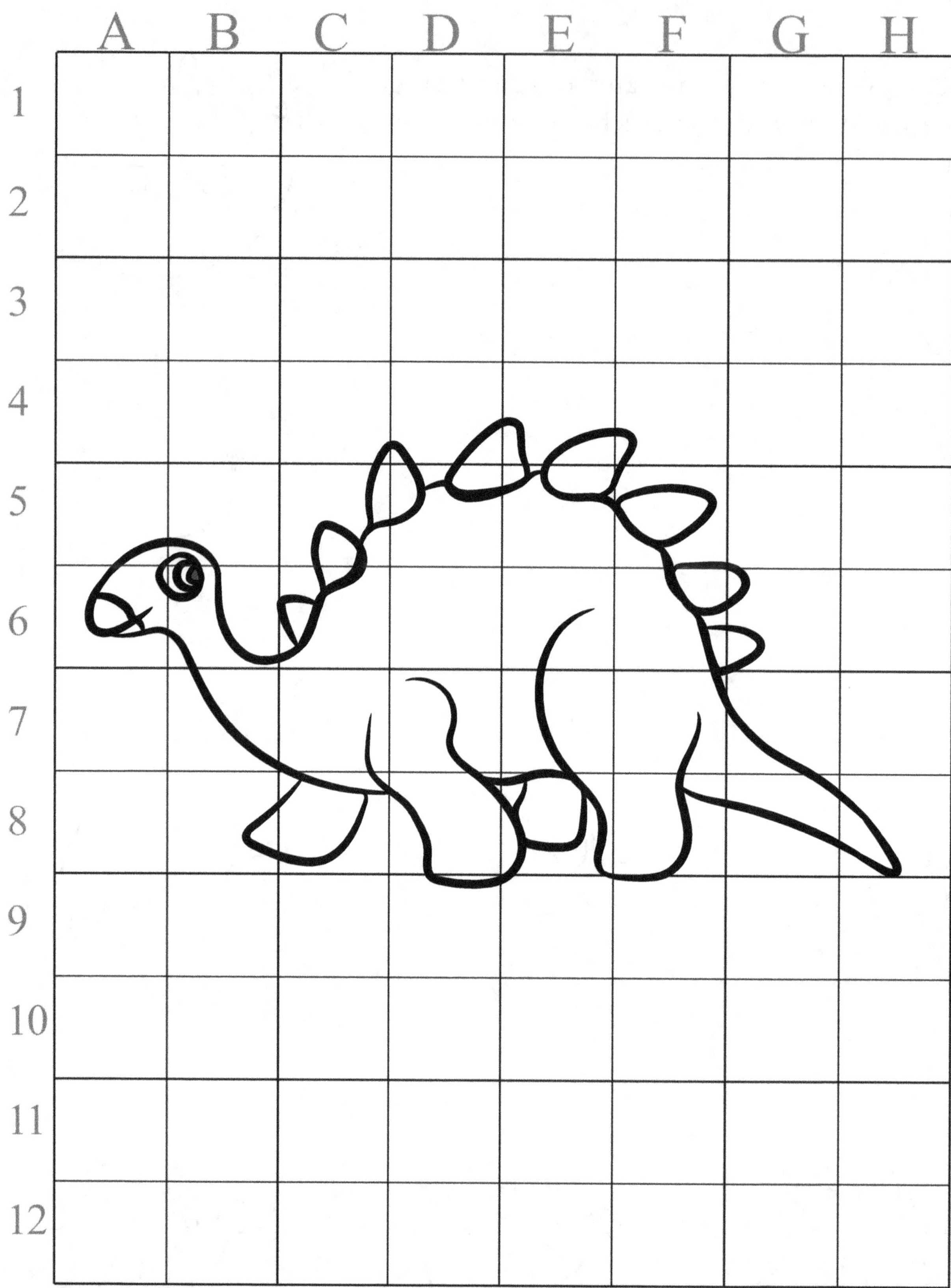

24. How to draw a dinosaur. You can make your dinosaur more cartoon like by exaggerating the size of the eyes. Begin your dinosaur by drawing a large eye and work around it to finish off your dinosaur.

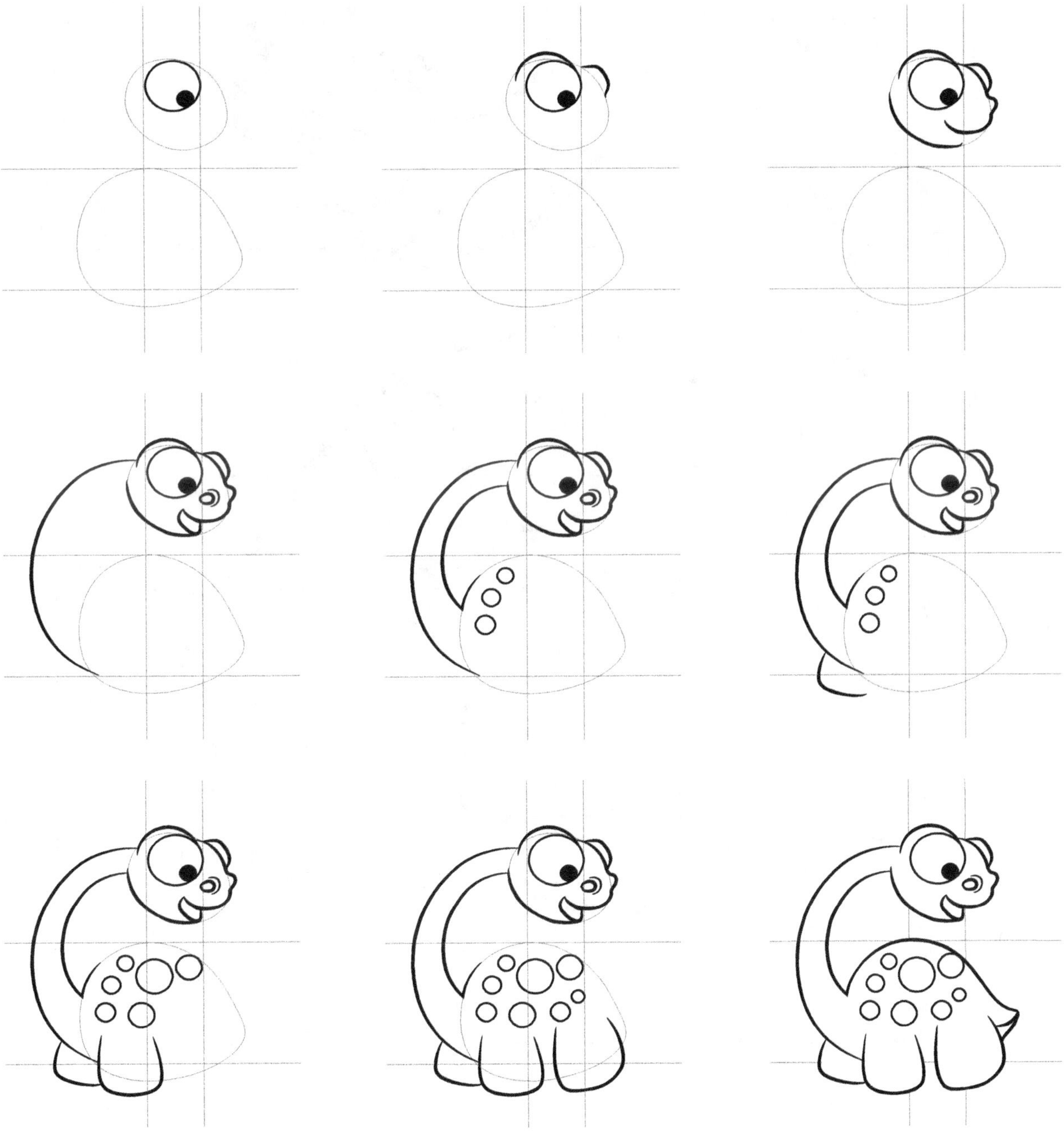

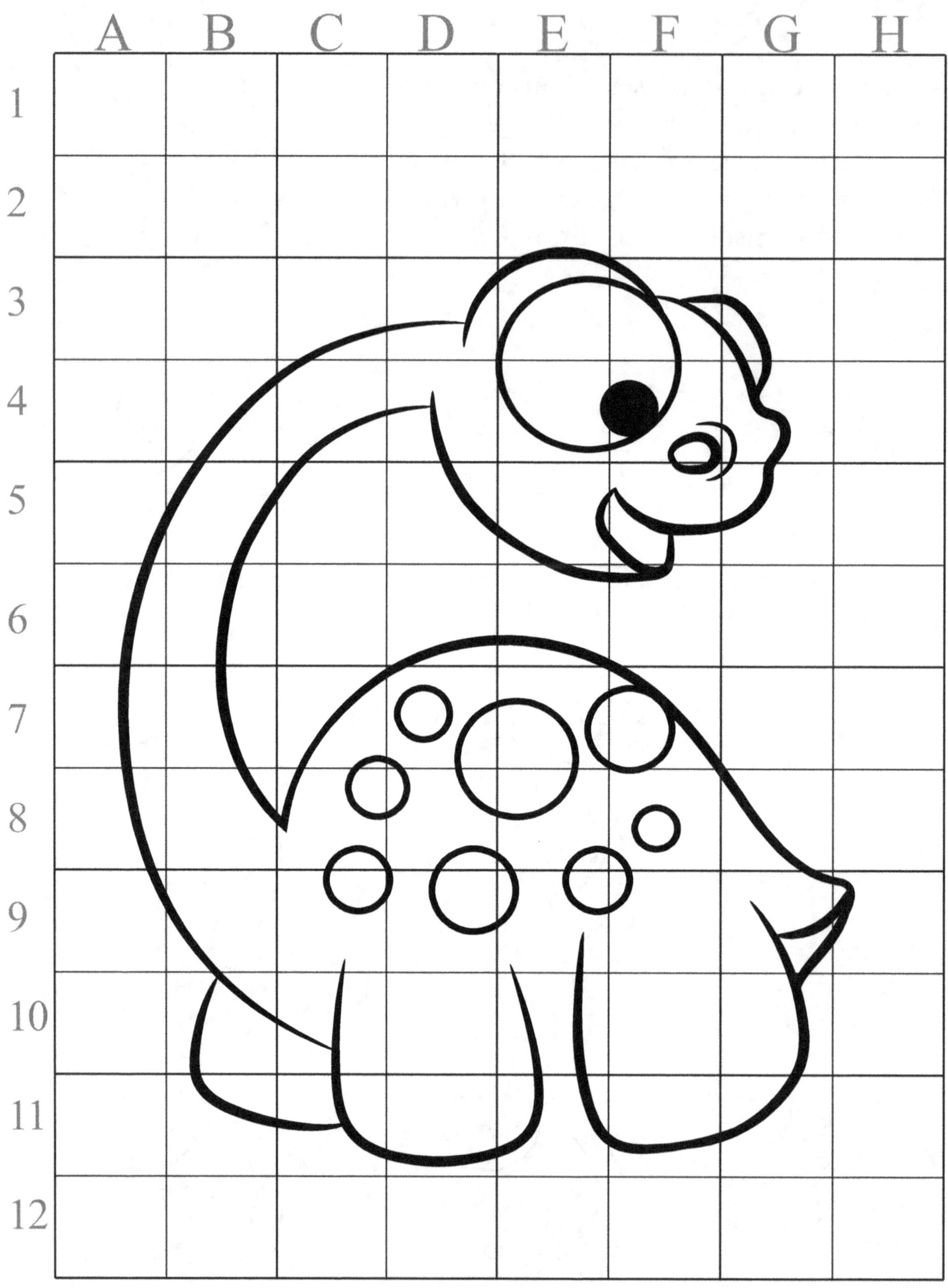

A B C D E F G H
1
2
3
4
5
6
7
8
9
10
11
12

25. How to draw a dinosaur. You can add lots of extra details to your dinosaur, such as spots and ridges.

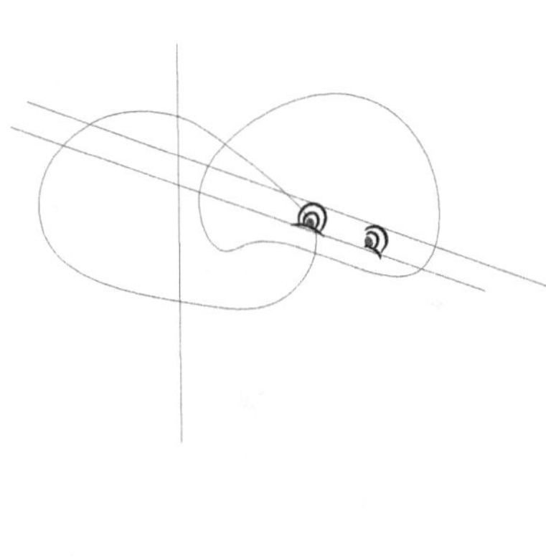

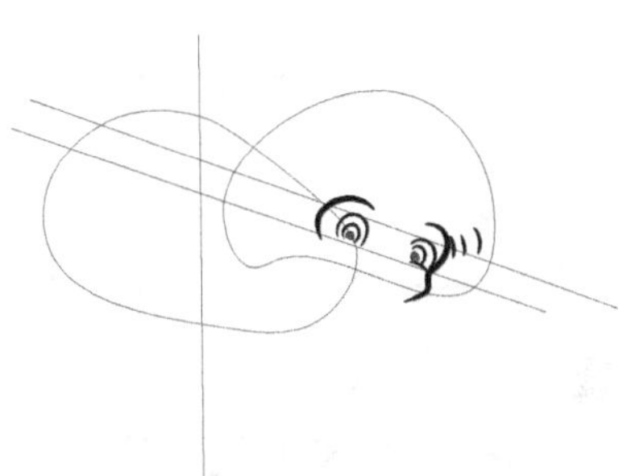

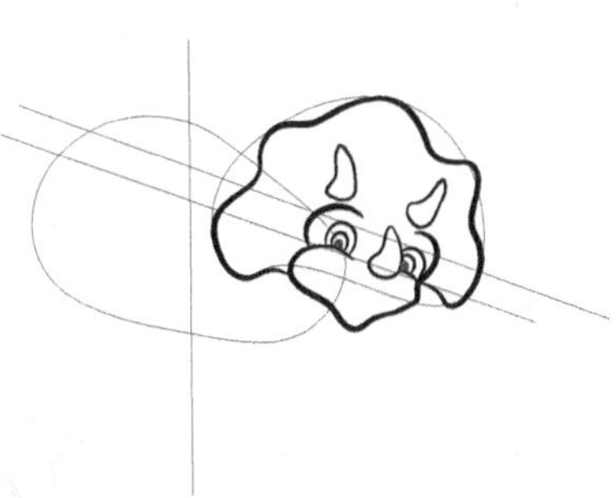

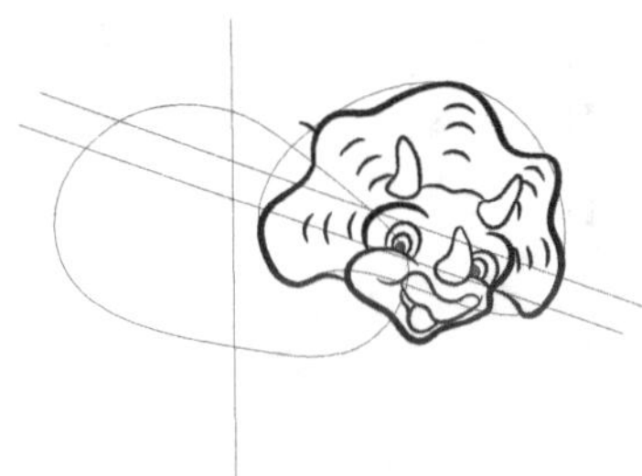

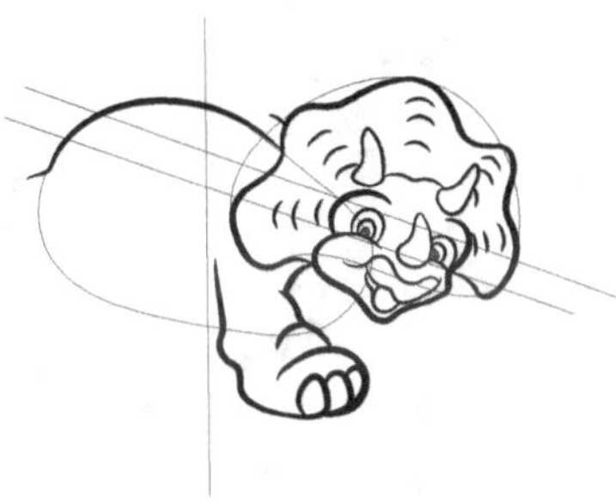

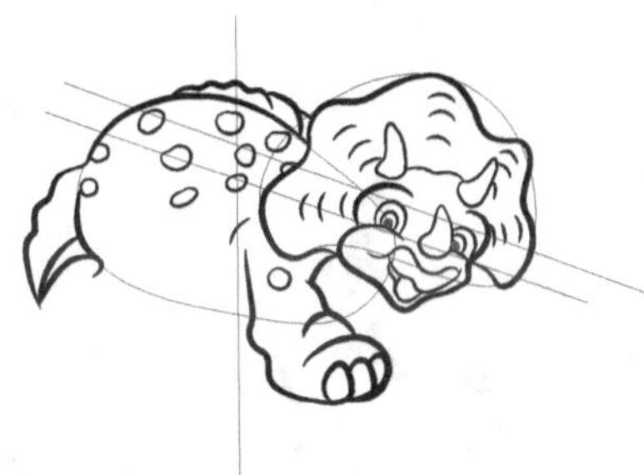

A B C D E F G H
1
2
3
4
5
6
7
8
9
10
11
12

26. Drawing dinosaurs with long necks. You can decide using a grid where to place your dinosaur's head in relation to the main part of its body. Use ellipses to guide you.

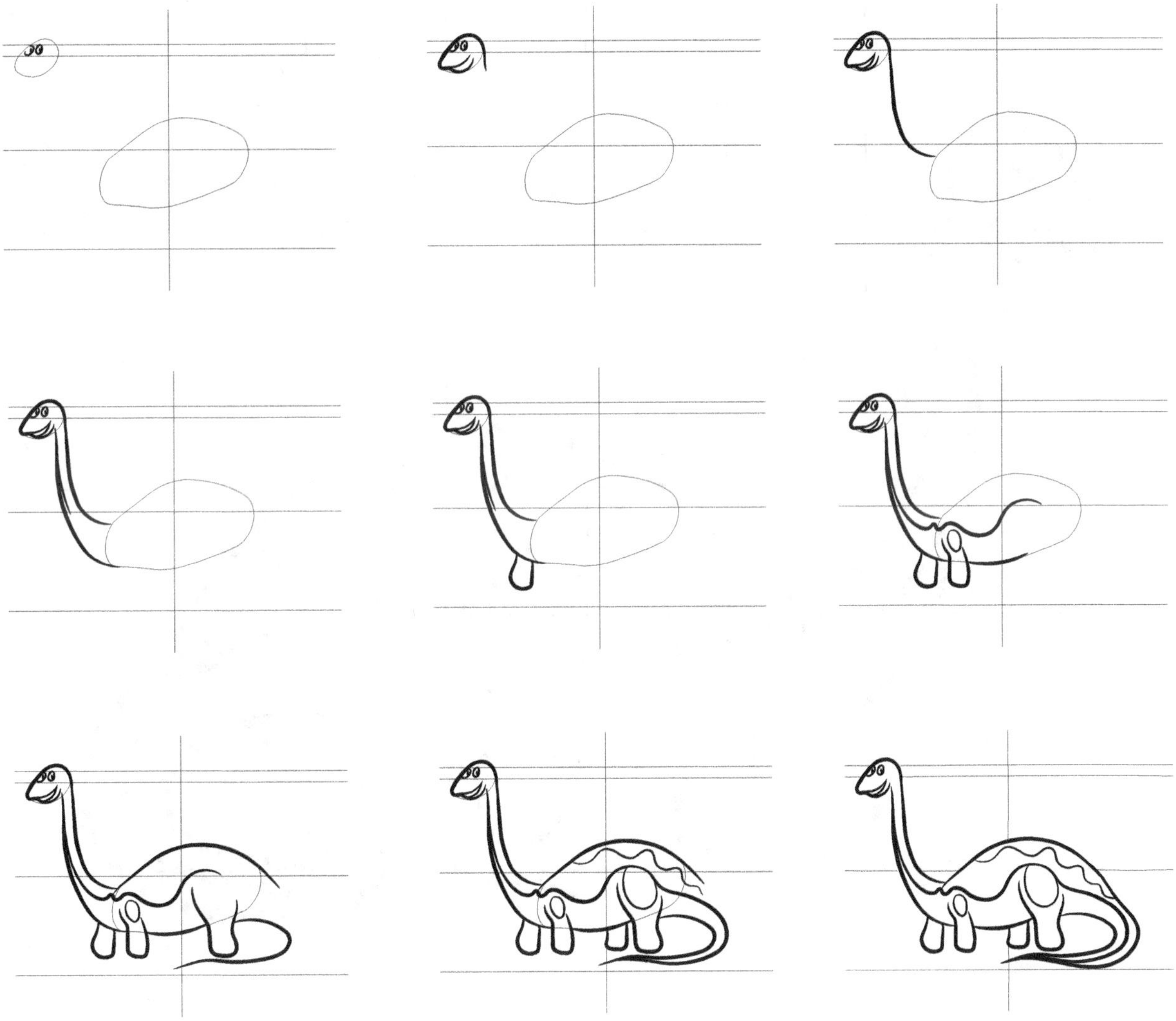

A B C D E F G H
1
2
3
4
5
6
7
8
9
10
11
12

27. How to draw a dinosaur. You can add
ridges to your dinosaur body to make it look
more unique.

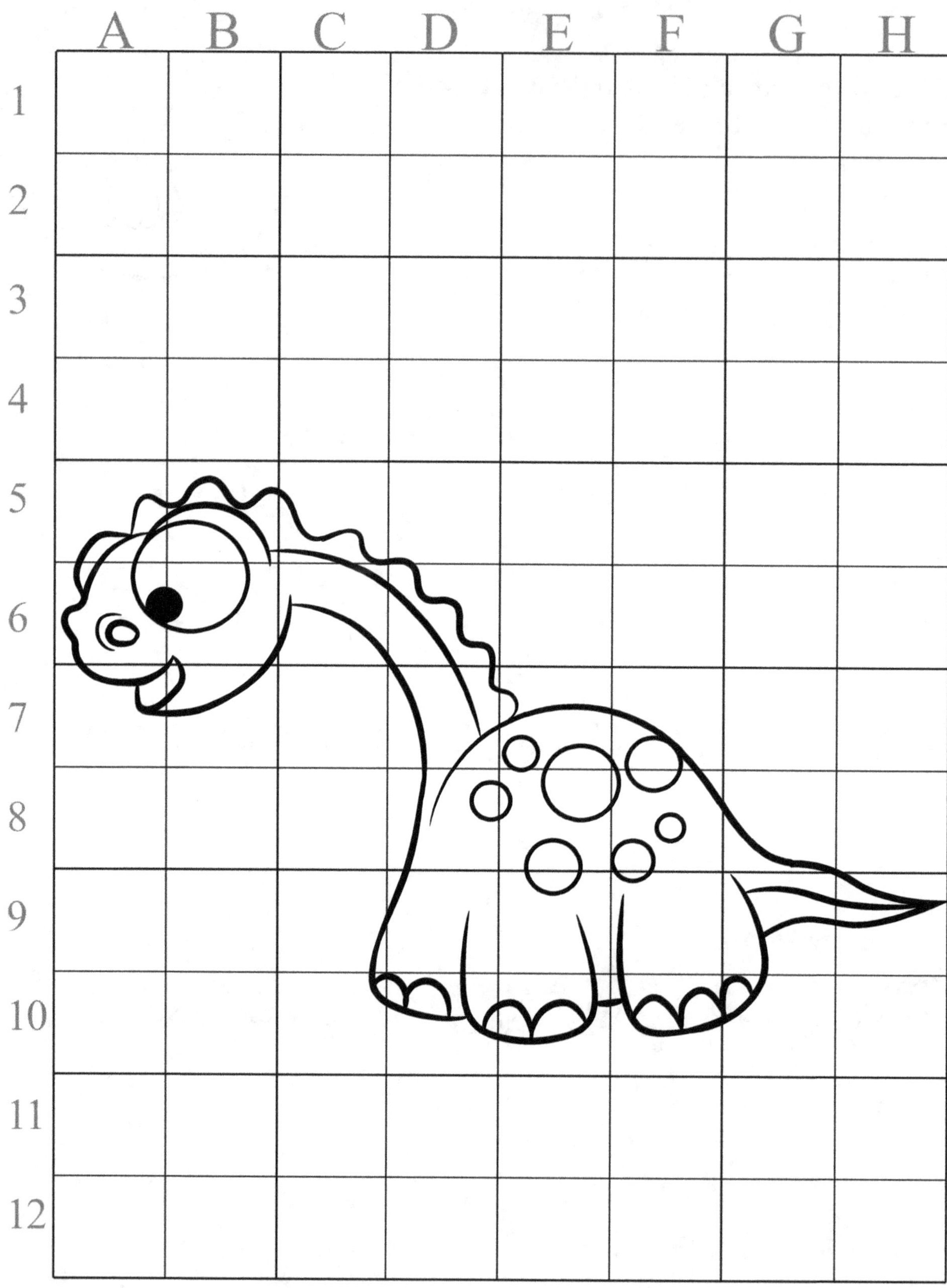

A B C D E F G H
1
2
3
4
5
6
7
8
9
10
11
12

28. How to draw a dinosaur. When drawing a flying dinosaur adding a triangle to your grid will help you to draw its wings.

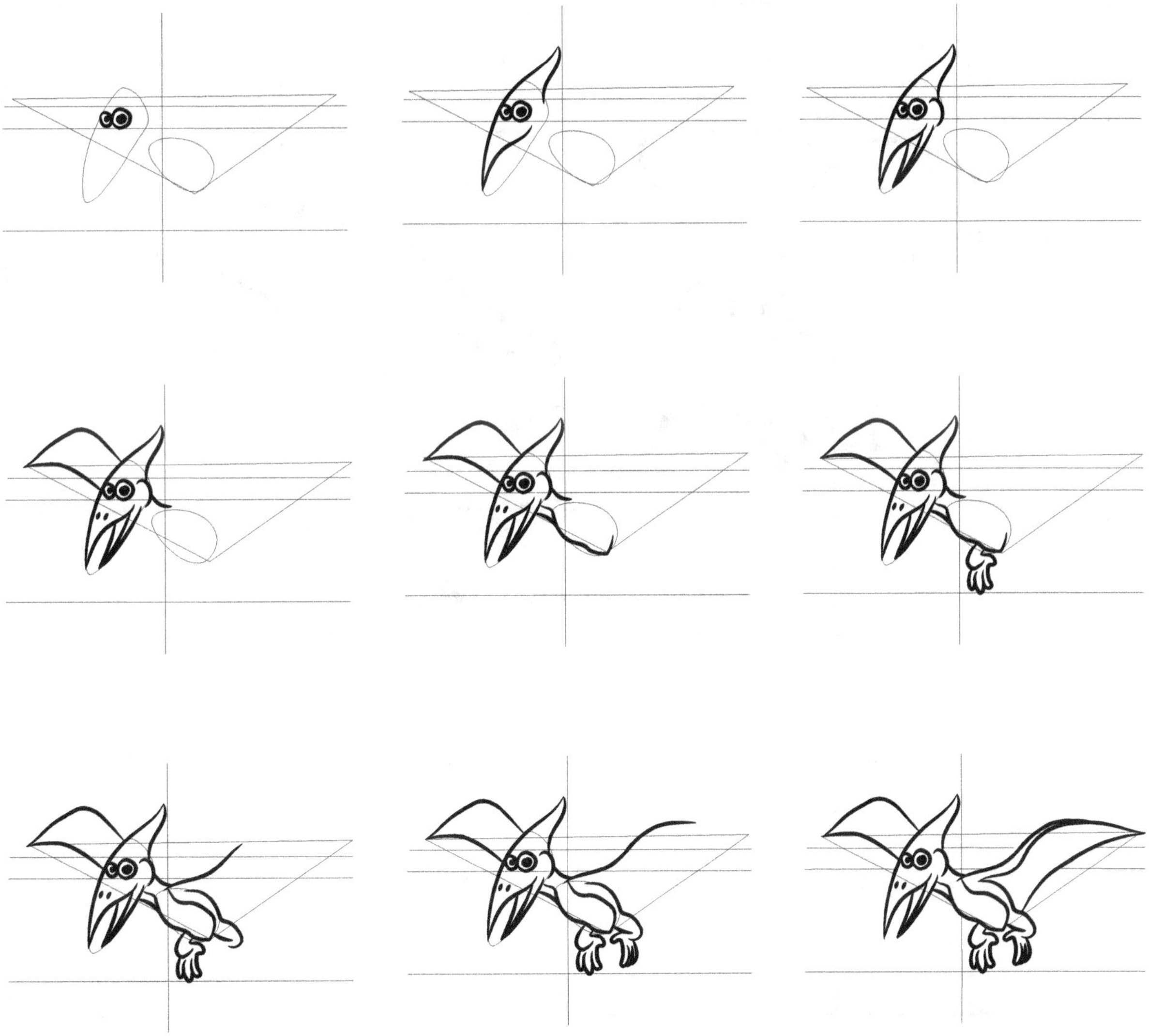

A B C D E F G H
1
2
3
4
5
6
7
8
9
10
11
12

29. How to draw a dinosaur. Begin you
dinosaur by drawing its eyes. You can make
your dinosaur short or long-necked by
changing the distance between the two
ellipses on your initial grid.

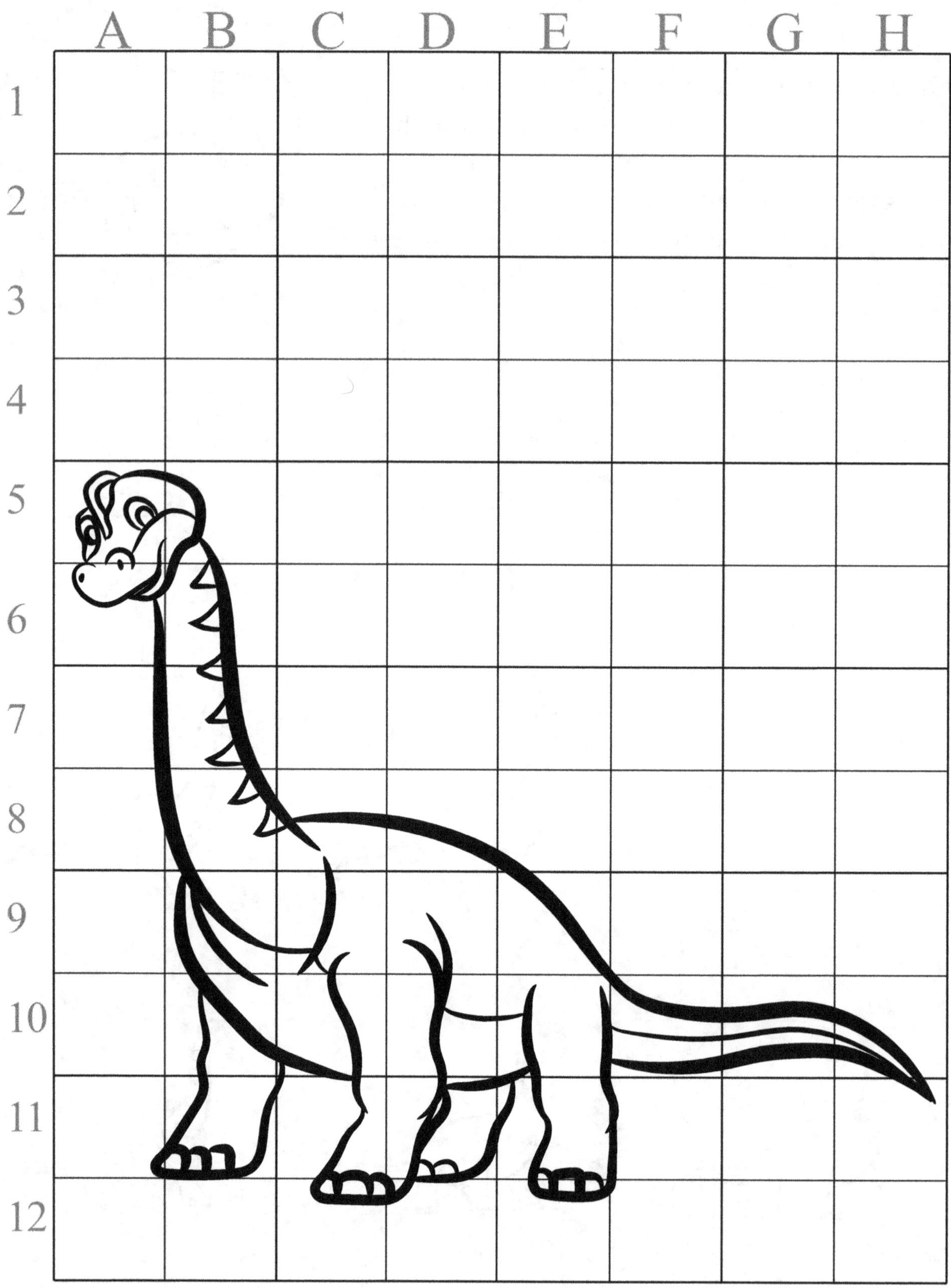

30. How to draw a dinosaur. You can change the position of your dinosaur's wings by altering the width of your triangle on your grid.

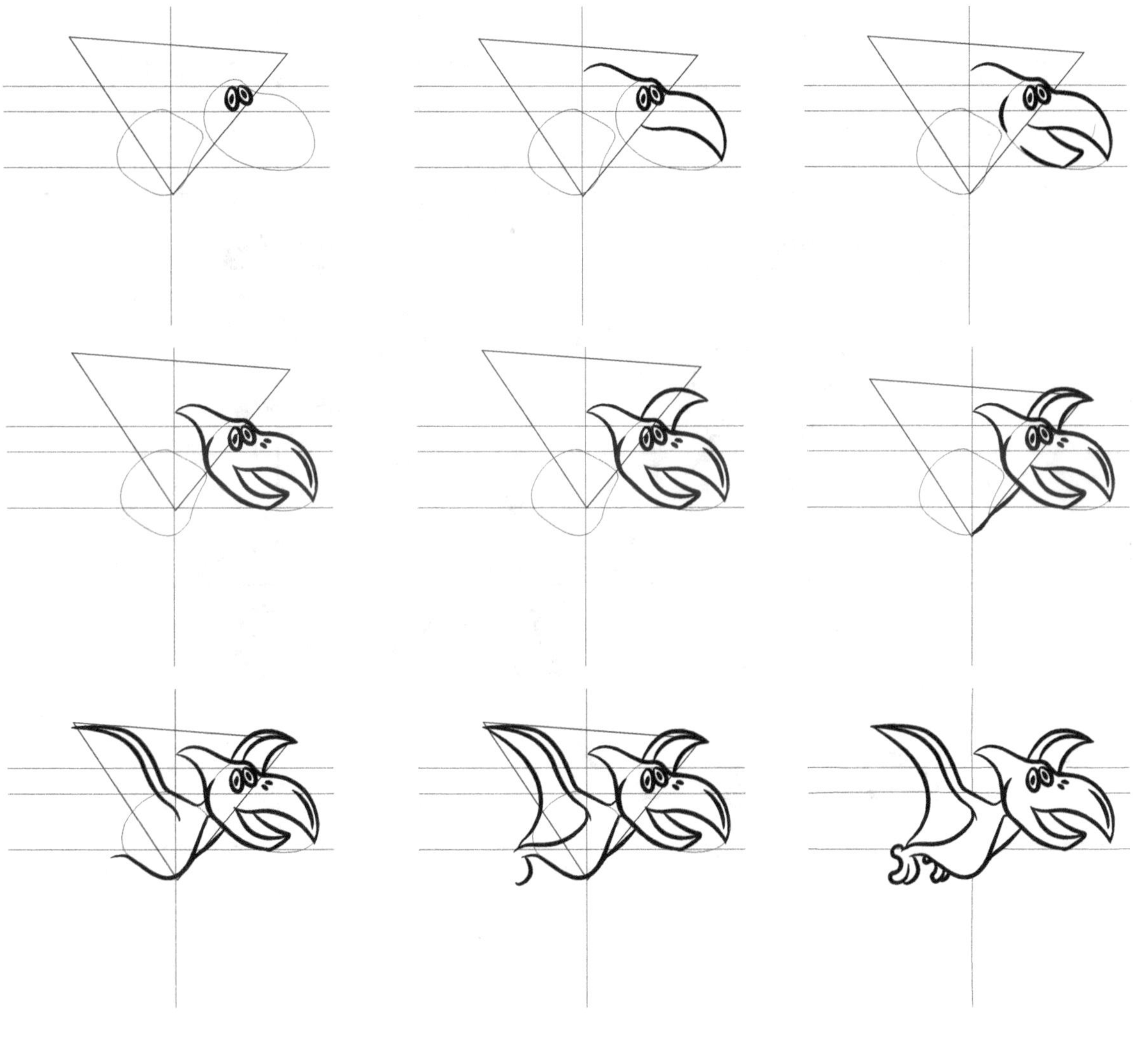

A B C D E F G H
1
2
3
4
5
6
7
8
9
10
11
12

31. How to draw a dinosaur. A triangle in your grid can help you set the direction of your flying dinosaur.

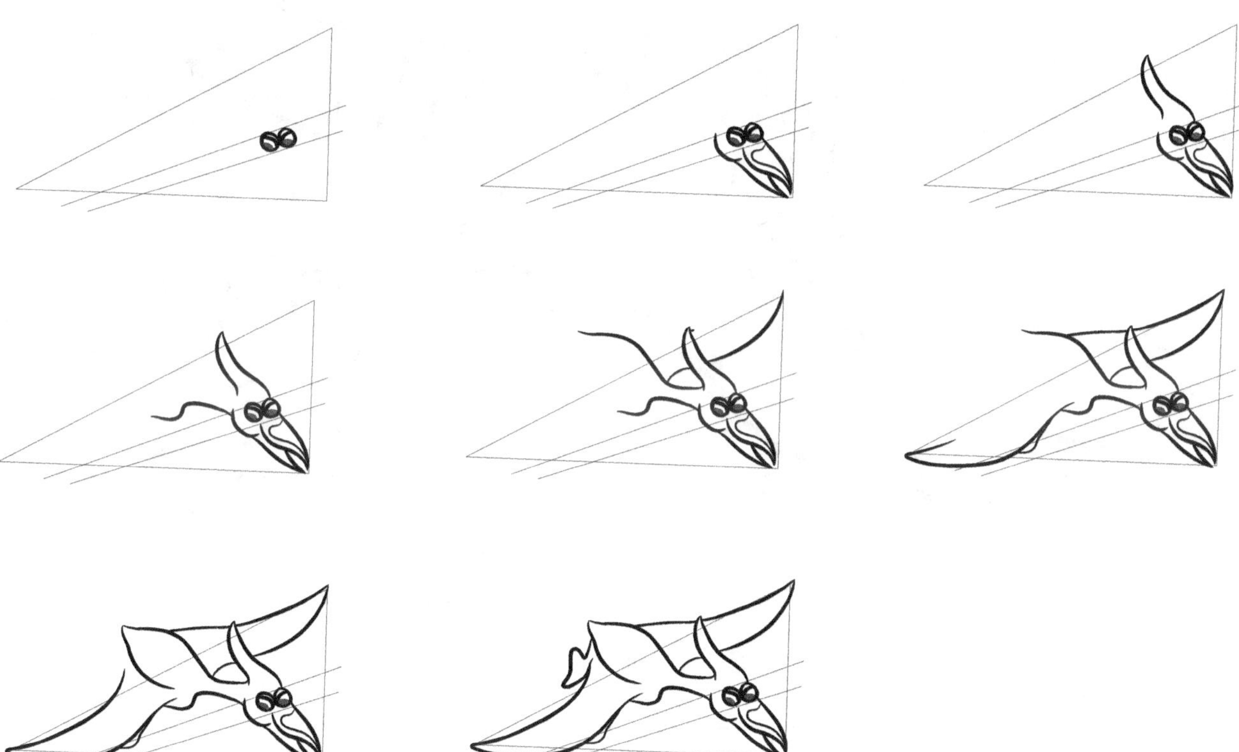

A B C D E F G H
1
2
3
4
5
6
7
8
9
10
11
12

32. How to draw a running dinosaur. Set
the position of your dinosaur by drawing a
line between your dinosaur's nose and its
back foot.

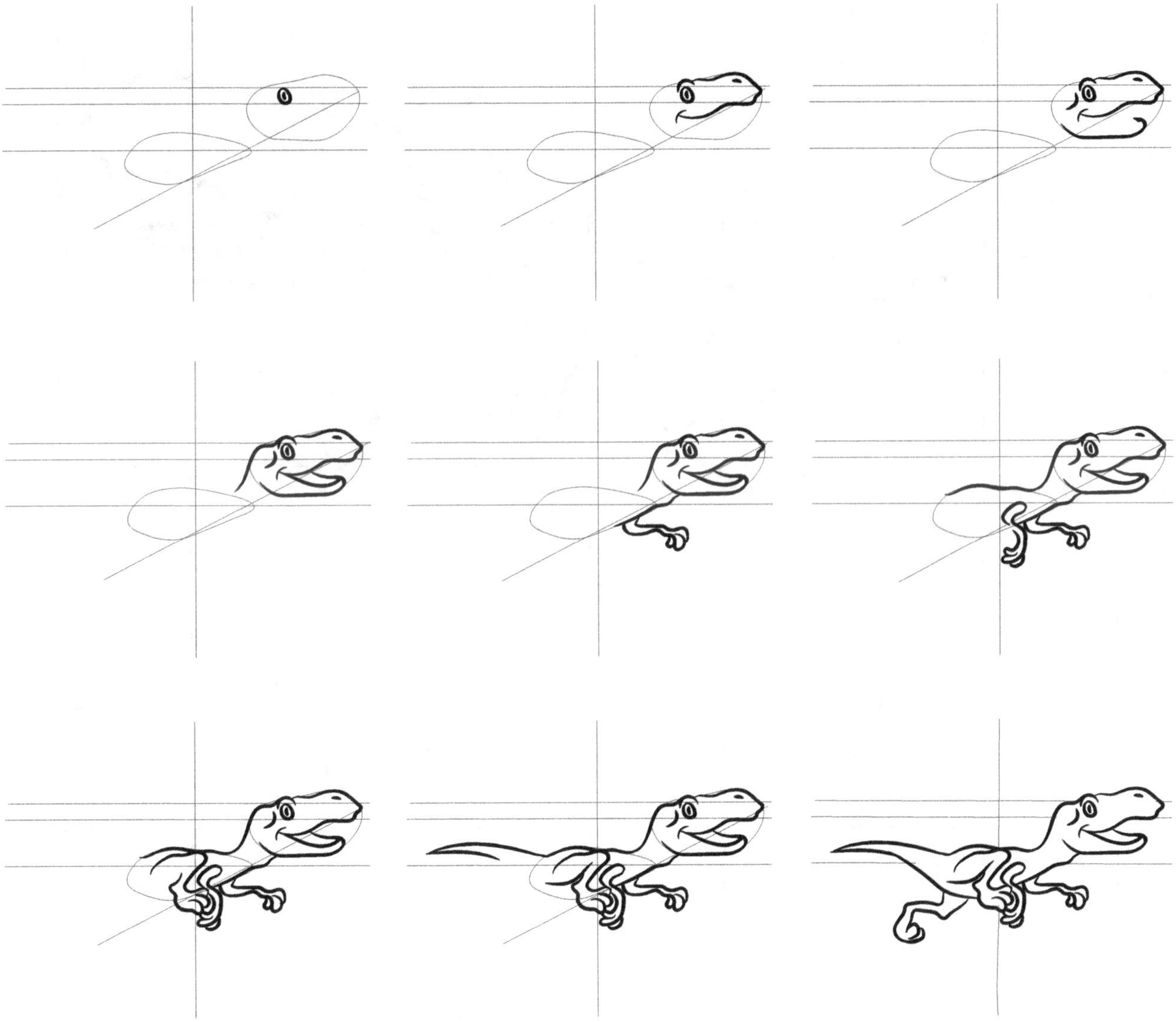

A B C D E F G H
1
2
3
4
5
6
7
8
9
10
11
12

33. How to draw a dinosaur. A simple grid can often help to guide you when drawing a dinosaur. Begin with the eyes.

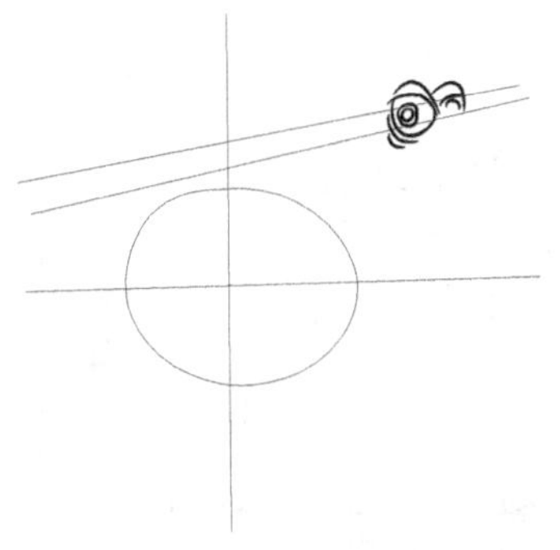
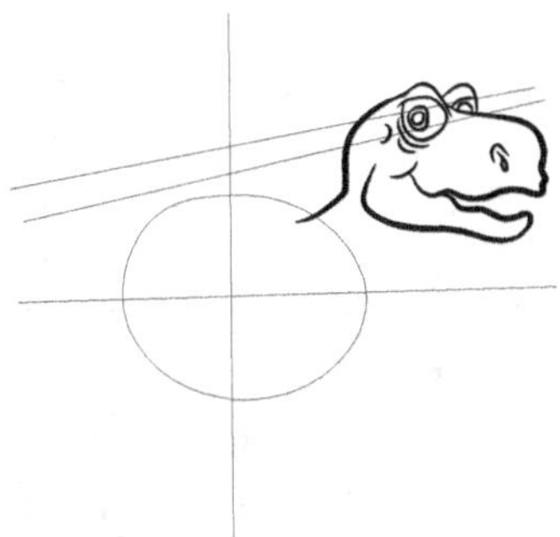
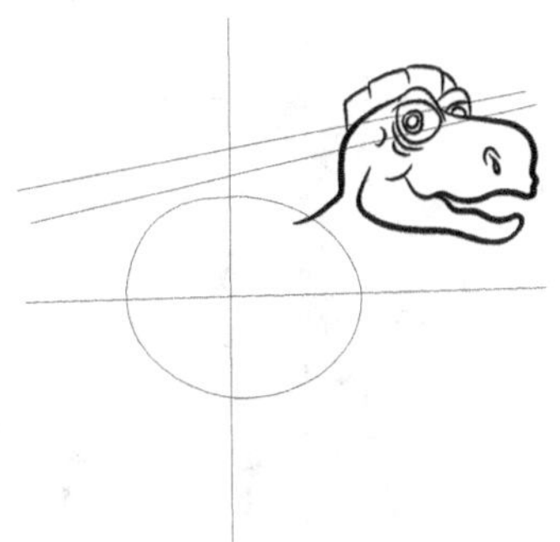

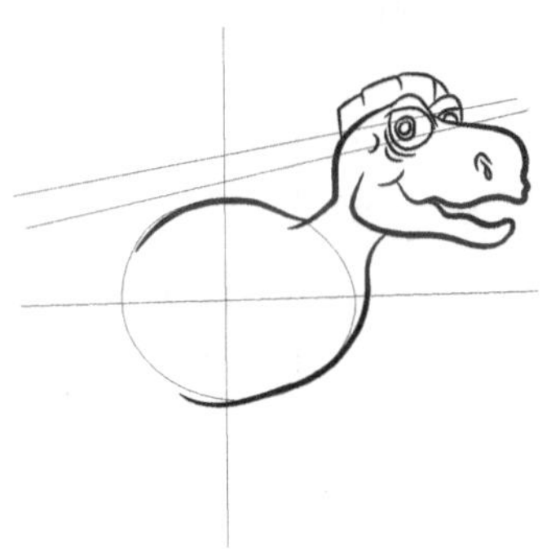

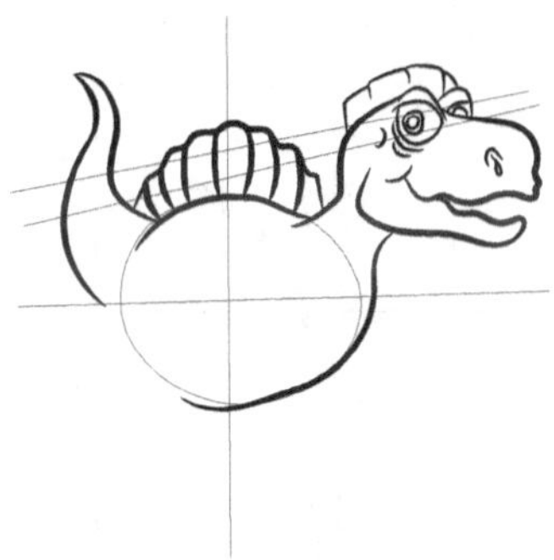

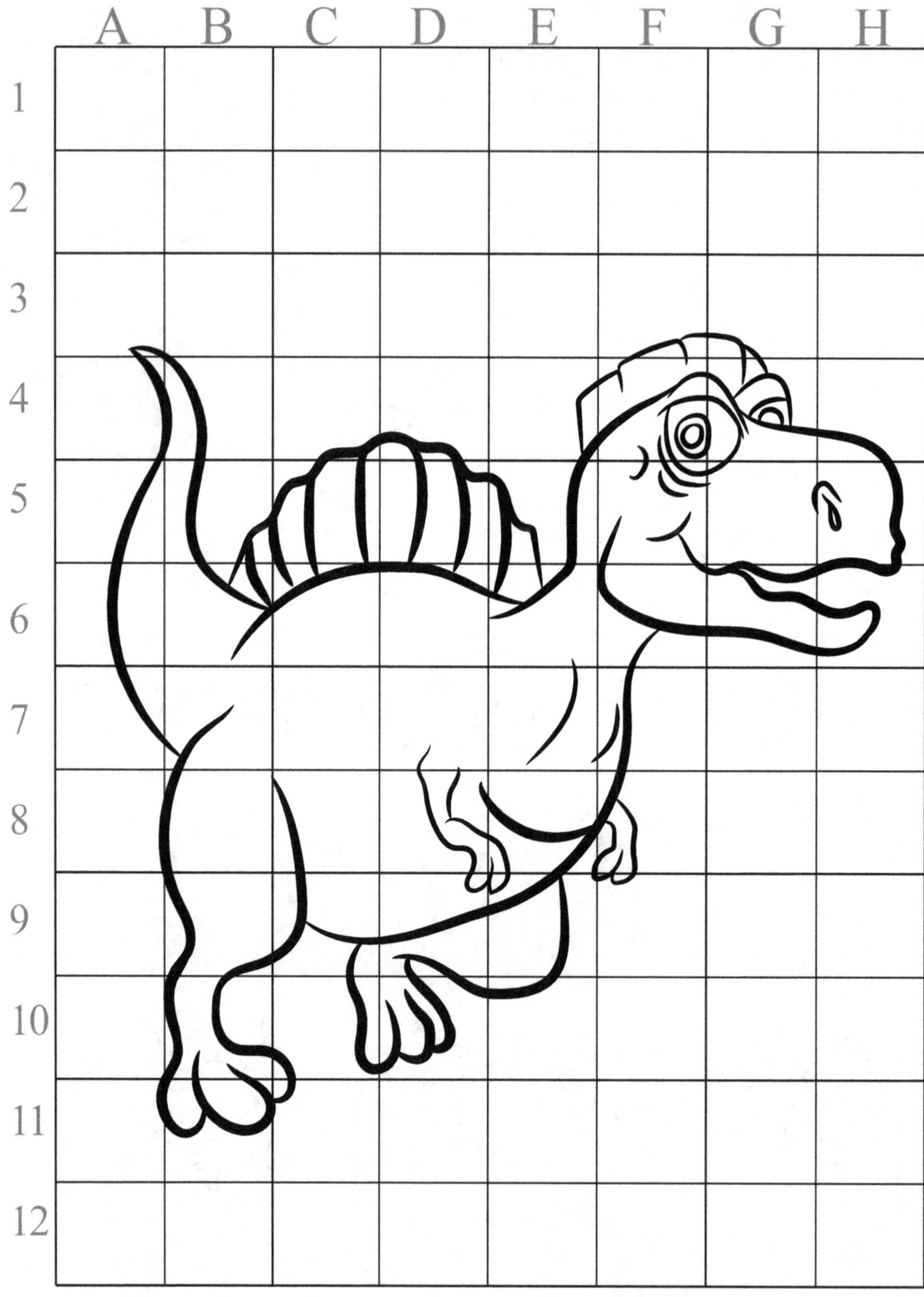

A B C D E F G H
1
2
3
4
5
6
7
8
9
10
11
12

34. How to draw a long-necked dinosaur. If you want your dinosaur to have a longer neck, extend the length between your ellipses on the grid.

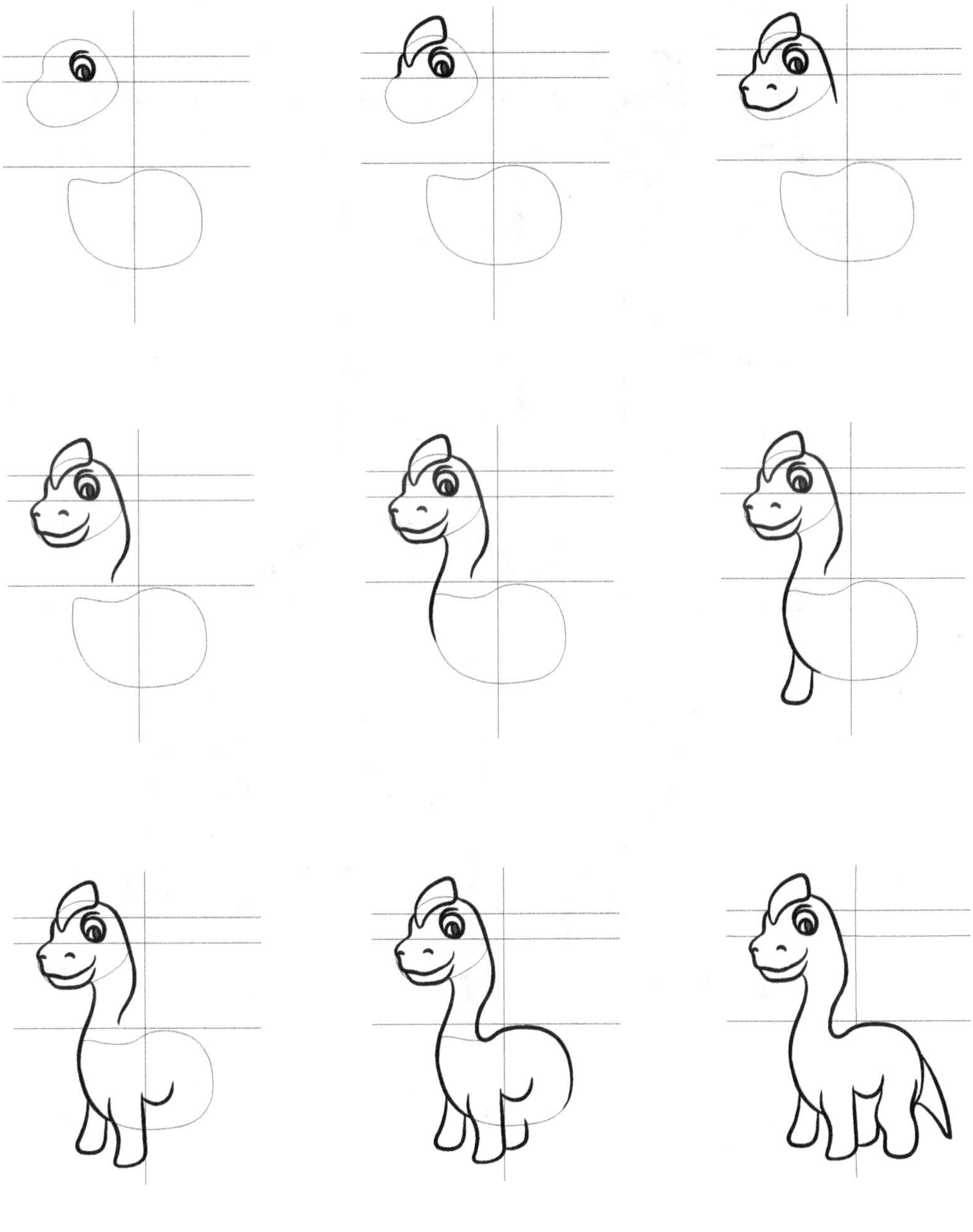

A B C D E F G H
1
2
3
4
5
6
7
8
9
10
11
12

35. A diagonal line on your grid layout can be very helpful if your dinosaur is leaning forwards.

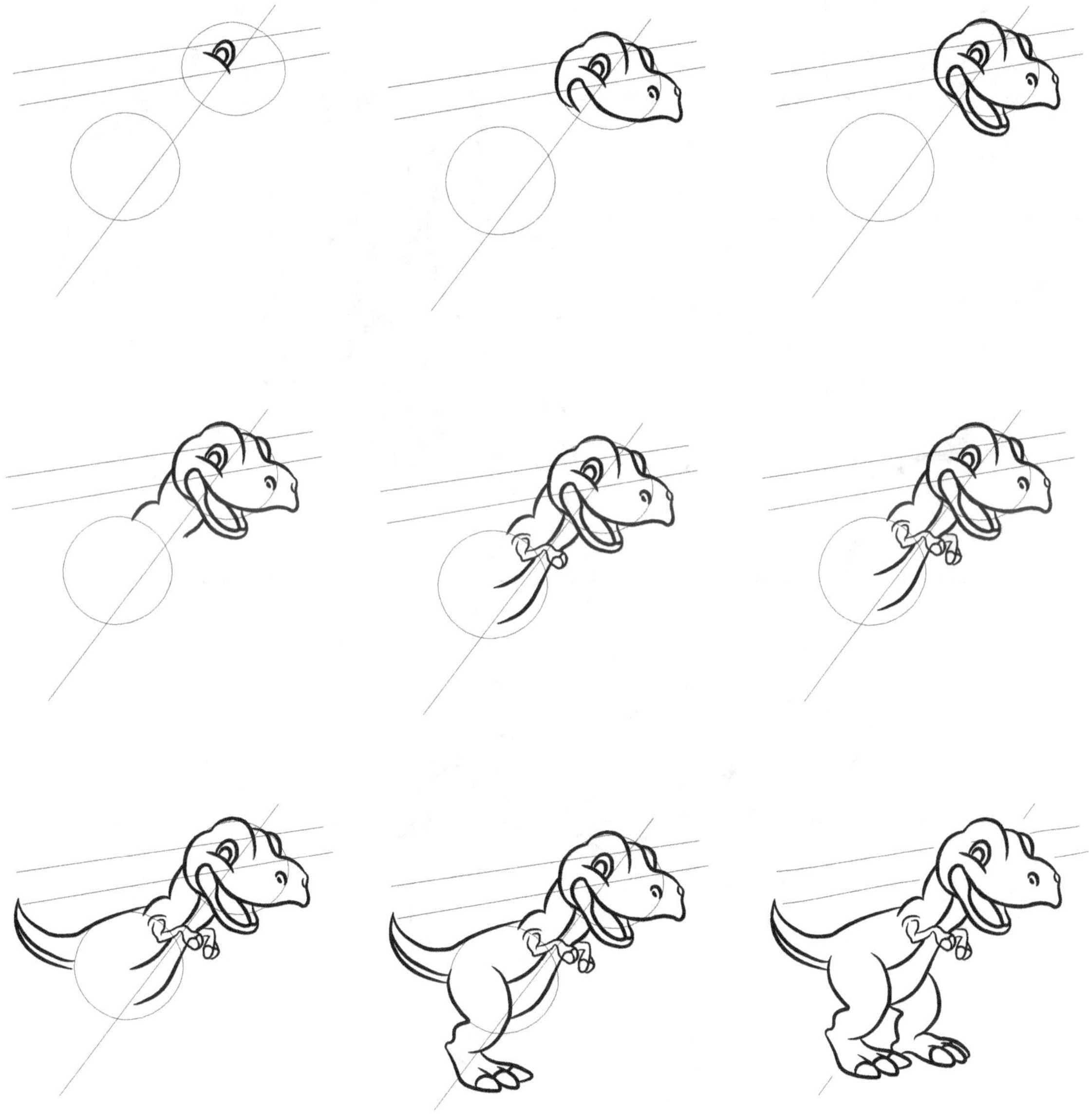

A B C D E F G H
1 2 3 4 5 6 7 8 9 10 11 12

36. A triangle on your grid can be very helpful in keeping the proportions of your dinosaur correct.

 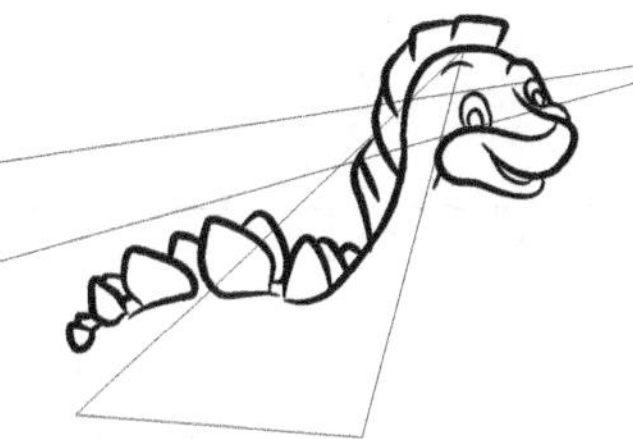

A B C D E F G H
1 2 3 4 5 6 7 8 9 10 11 12

37. Using ellipses to guide the shape of your dinosaur's body can be very helpful.

A B C D E F G H
1
2
3
4
5
6
7
8
9
10
11
12

38. How to draw a simple dinosaur. On your grid you can add an arc to help guide you with the curve of your dinosaur's tail.

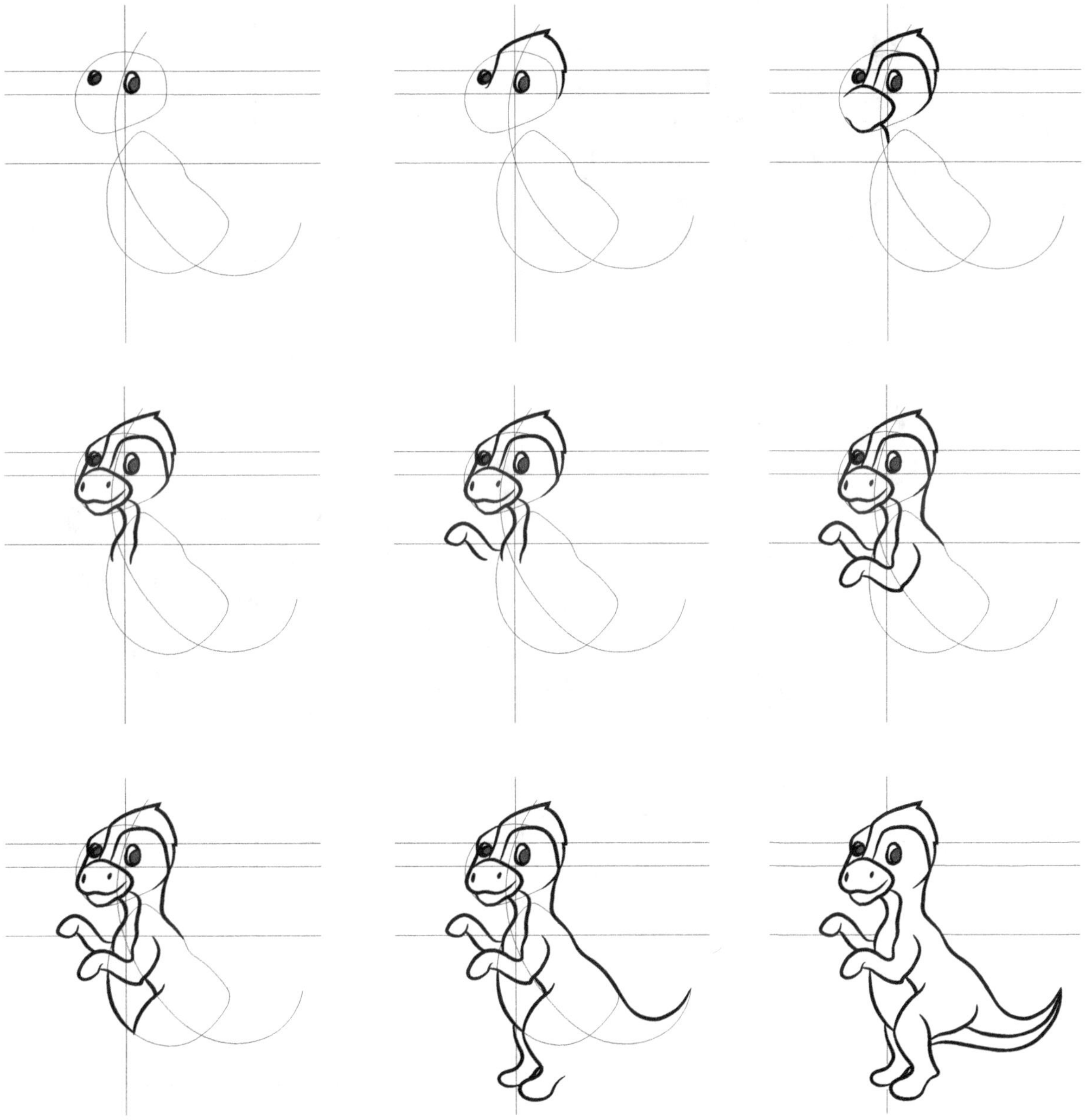

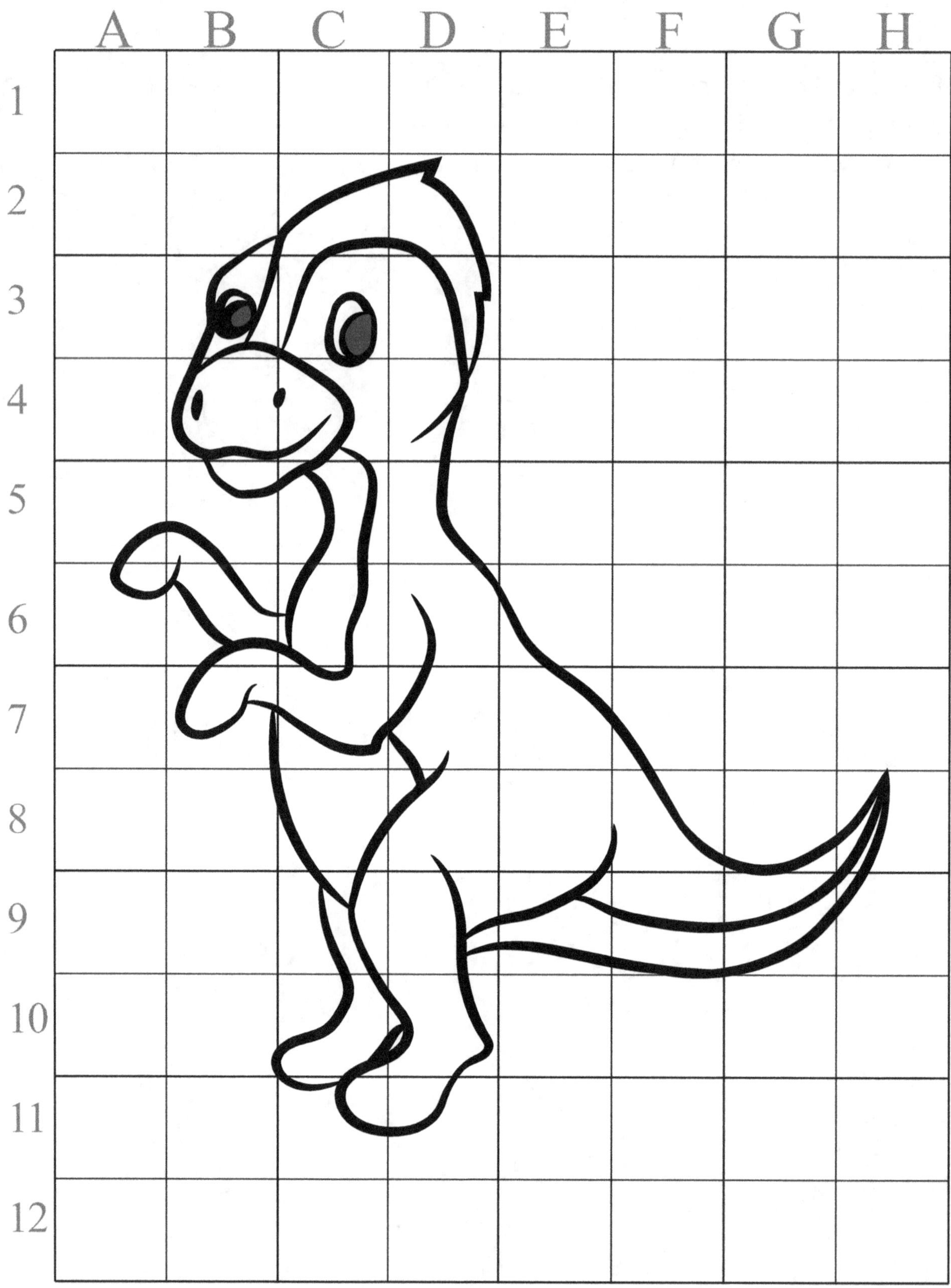

A B C D E F G H
1
2
3
4
5
6
7
8
9
10
11
12

www.ingramcontent.com/pod-product-compliance
Lightning Source LLC
Chambersburg PA
CBHW081156130726
47996CB00009B/3142